The Kite Runner

A Portrait of the Marc Forster Film

Screenplay by David BENIOFF

Based on the Novel by KHALED HOSSEINI

Foreword by KHALED HOSSEINI

A NEWMARKET PICTORIAL MOVIEBOOK

NEWMARKET PRESS • NEW YORK

Afghan Rug art courtesy of ABC Carpet & Home,
a long-time supporter of Afghanistan's culture and art, www.abchome.com

This book is published simultaneously in the United States of America and in Canada. All rights reserved. This book may
not be reproduced, in whole or in part, in any form, without written permission. Inquiries should be addressed to:
Permissions Department, Newmarket Press, 18 East 48th Street, New York, NY 10017.

FIRST EDITION

10 9 8 7 6 5 4 3 2 1
ISBN: 978-1-55704-801-1 (paperback)

10 9 8 7 6 5 4 3 2 1
ISBN: 978-1-55704-804-2 (hardcover)

Library of Congress Catalog-in-Publication Data available upon request.

QUANTITY PURCHASES
Companies, professional groups, clubs, and other organizations may qualify for special terms when ordering quantities of
this title. For information, write to Special Sales, Newmarket Press, 18 East 48th Street, New York, NY 10017;
call (212) 832-3575 or 1-800-669-3903; FAX (212) 832-3629; or e-mail info@newmarketpress.com.

www.newmarketpress.com

Manufactured in the United States of America.

Special thanks to editor Linda Sunshine and Timothy Shaner at Night and Day Design (nightanddaydesign.biz).

Produced by Newmarket Press: Esther Margolis, President and Publisher; Frank DeMaio, Production Director; Keith
Hollaman, Executive Editor; Linda Carbone, Editor; Paul Sugarman, Digital Supervisor

Other Newmarket Pictorial Moviebooks and Newmarket Insider Film Books include:

*The Art of The Matrix**
*The Art of X2**
The Art of X-Men: The Last Stand
*Bram Stoker's Dracula: The Film and the Legend**
*Chicago: The Movie and Lyrics**
*Dances with Wolves: The Illustrated Story of the Epic Film**
Dreamgirls
*E.T. The Extra-Terrestrial: From Concept to Classic**
Gladiator: The Making of the Ridley Scott Epic Film
*Good Night, and Good Luck: The Screenplay and
History Behind the Landmark Movie**

*Hotel Rwanda: Bringing the True Story of an African Hero to Film**
The Jaws Log
Memoirs of a Geisha: A Portrait of the Film
The Namesake: A Portrait of the Film by Mira Nair
*Ray: A Tribute to the Movie, the Music, and the Man**
Rescue Me: Uncensored
Rush Hour 1, 2, 3: Lights, Camera, Action!
Saving Private Ryan: The Men, The Mission, The Movie
Schindler's List: Images of the Steven Spielberg Film
*Superbad: The Illustrated Moviebook**
Tim Burton's Corpse Bride: An Invitation to the Wedding

*Includes screenplay.

Contents

There is a way
to be good again...

Foreword

by Khaled Hosseini

Above: Production design by Carlos Conti; graphic illustration by Maud Gircourt.

One chilly morning in November of 2006, I stood beside my father and watched an actor peek through a set of metallic gates. We were in the city of Kashgar in western China, on the set of *The Kite Runner,* Marc Forster's film based on David Benioff's adaptation of my first novel. The actor was Khalid Abdalla, who plays Amir, the fallible, guilt-ridden central character. Amir has come back to Kabul after a two-decade-long absence. While he was away, wars have swept through Afghanistan, a million people have died, countless have been displaced, and the country has fallen into the hands of the brutal Taliban regime. Now, Amir has come home to rescue a boy he has never met, but also to exorcise deeply personal demons and rescue himself, as he sees it, from damnation.

Watching Khalid Abdalla/Amir peeking sadly through the gates at the house where he was raised in the 1970s echoed with me in strange and almost disorienting ways. Like Amir, I too was born in Kabul in the mid-1960s, lived there in the 1970s, and came to the San Francisco Bay Area in the early 1980s to begin a new life as an immigrant. I too was away while Afghanistan was destroyed. And like Amir, I too went back to Kabul as a grown man to revisit the land of my childhood.

In March of 2003, with the novel three months away from publication, I found myself tracing Amir's footsteps, sitting in the window seat of an Ariana Airlines Boeing 727 headed toward Kabul. The last time I had seen Kabul, I was an eleven-year-old, thin-framed seventh grader. I was going back now as a thirty-eight-year-old physician, writer, husband, and father of two. I remember gazing out the window, waiting for the plane to break through the clouds, waiting for Kabul to appear below me. When it did, a few lines from *The Kite Runner* came to me, and Amir's thoughts suddenly became my own: "The kinship I felt suddenly for the old land . . . it surprised me. . . . I thought I had forgotten about this land. But I hadn't. Maybe Afghanistan hadn't forgotten me either." The old adage in writing is to write about what you have experienced. I was going to experience what I had already written about.

Given this unusual circumstance, my two-week stay in Kabul took on a surreal quality. Every day, I saw places and things I had seen months before with Amir's eyes. Walking through the crowded streets of Kabul for the first time, I was buoyed, like Amir, with a sense of coming home to an old friend. But also like Amir, I felt like a tourist in my own country. We'd both been away a long time. Neither one of us had fought in the wars; neither one of us had bled with the Afghan people. I had written about Amir's guilt. Now I tasted it.

Soon the line between Amir's memories and my own began to blur.

Amir had lived out my memories on the pages of *The Kite Runner*. In Kabul, I found myself living out his. When I was driven through the once beautiful, now war-ravaged Jadeh-maywand Avenue, past collapsed buildings, piles of rubble, and bullet-pocked, roofless walls where beggars took shelter, I remembered my father buying me rosewater ice cream there in the early 1970s. And I remembered that Amir and his loving servant, Hassan, used to buy their kites on this same street, from a blind old man named Saifo. I sat on the crumbling steps of Cinema Park, where my brother and I used to watch free undubbed Russian films in the winters, and where Amir and Hassan had seen their favorite film, *The Magnificent Seven,* no fewer than thirteen times. With Amir, I passed by smoke-filled, tiny kabob houses where our fathers—Amir's Baba and mine—used to take us, where sweaty men still sat cross-legged

From Left: Author Khaled Hosseini with actors Homayoun Ershadi, Shaun Toub, and Khalid Abdalla.

9

behind charcoal grills and feverishly fanned skewers of sizzling chopan kabob. Together we gazed up at sky over the gardens of the sixteenth-century emperor Babur, and spotted a kite floating over the city.

I thought of a sunny winter day in 1975, the day of the kite-fighting tournament. That was the fateful day when twelve-year-old Amir betrayed his adoring friend Hassan, the day that would draw him back to Afghanistan years later to seek atonement for his weaknesses. And as I sat on a bench at Ghazi Stadium and watched the New Year's Day parade with thousands of Afghans, I thought of my father and me watching a game of Buzkashi there in 1973. But I also thought of Amir, who had witnessed the Taliban stone a pair of adulterers in this same stadium, a scene rendered in Marc Forster's film with naked, unflinching brutality. That was at the south end goalpost, where now a group of young men in traditional garments was dancing the traditional atan dance in a circle.

But perhaps nowhere did fiction and life collide more dizzyingly than when I found my father's old house in the Wazir Akbar Khan neighborhood, the house where I was raised in the 1970s. It took me three days of searching—I had no address and the neighborhood had changed drastically—but I kept looking until I spotted the familiar arch over the gates.

I peeked through the metallic gates. In a way, I had already been there. Months before, I had stood beside Amir at the gates of his Baba's house—now overtaken by murderous Taliban soldiers—and felt his loss. I had watched him set his hands on the rusty wrought-iron bars, and together we had gazed at the sagging roof, the broken windows, and crumbling front steps. Eerily, my father's house resembled Amir and Baba's old house. It too was the picture of fallen splendor. The paint had faded, the grass had withered, the trees were gone, and the walls were crumbling. And like Amir, I was struck by how much smaller the house was in reality than the version that had for so long lived in my memories.

And here I was now, three years later, on a movie

set in China, watching Khalid Abdalla/Amir stepping through those gates, fusing my own past and present, my own reality and fiction. The sadness, the passage of time, and the sense of loss materialized on Khalid Abdalla's face. And echoed in my own mind all over again. I had written this scene, I had lived it, and now I was watching it performed before me.

Soon, across screens throughout the world, millions of people will stand beside Amir and peek through those gates. They will feel his loss. What they may not know is that they are feeling mine as well. And in a way, that of countless other Afghans who have seen their homeland ravaged.

Today, Afghanistan is still trying to recover from nearly three decades of war, famine, drought, and massive human displacement and suffering. It cannot afford to be forgotten. It is my belief that Marc Forster's lyrical film, adapted with tenderness and affection by David Benioff, will make it difficult to forget about the Afghan people. Marc's film brings to life the forgotten, more innocent days of the pre-Soviet era, the struggles of the Afghan immigrants living abroad, fallen from grace, and the endless anguish of those who stayed behind and suffered at the hands of one unforgiving regime after another. It is my hope that this film—coming at a time when Afghanistan is fading again from the headlines—will bring back global attention to my homeland and to the needs of its vulnerable people. ■

The Making of The Kite Runner

From Bestselling Book to Epic Film

In 2003, Khaled Hosseini's *The Kite Runner* shot to the top of bestseller lists around the globe, selling over eight million copies in more than 34 countries. Written by a physician born in Afghanistan who, like his lead character, came to America as a boy and didn't return for decades, *The Kite Runner* took readers on a journey, across continents, into one man's quest to right a terrible wrong that haunted him all his life. Though the story was fictional, Hosseini's intimate knowledge of growing up in Kabul when it was "the pearl of Central Asia," before the Soviet invasion and the rise of the Taliban, as well as his experiences emigrating as a young man to America, lent his story an authenticity and humanity that deeply affected readers.

"I'm continually astonished by how people have reacted to my novel," says Hosseini, "but I think it must be because there is a very intense emotional core to this story that people connect with. The themes of guilt, friendship, forgiveness, loss, the desire for atonement and to be better than who you think you are, are not Afghan themes but very human experiences, regardless of one's ethnic, cultural, or religious background."

It was these themes, long before the book was an international bestseller—in fact, when it was merely an obscure and as-yet-unpublished manuscript—that drew the attention of producers William Horberg and

Left: The sweeping vistas and vast mountain ranges of western China were the backdrop for The Kite Runner. *Right: Author Khaled Housseini (left) with lead actor Khalid Abdalla.*

Rebecca Yeldham. "It was one of the most powerful and cinematic pieces of literature that I'd ever read," says Yeldham. "It's a story that's told in the most lyrical, evocative, and beautiful way; as you're reading, you literally *see* its events unfold."

Bill Horberg was similarly inspired by the book. "Reading *The Kite Runner* was a wonderful experience," he says. "You go on a journey with these two boys, a journey into a culture, into a family and into redemption for the character of Amir."

Horberg and Yeldham brought the manuscript to the attention of Walter Parkes and Laurie MacDonald at DreamWorks, and the filmmakers joined forces to secure the rights to the forthcoming novel. For Parkes, the heart of the book lay in the mysterious, albeit fragile, bonds of childhood friendships. "I thought right away of my relationship with my best friend when I was 10 or 11 and the kind of private, extended fantasy world young boys occupy in their friendships," reflects Parkes. MacDonald adds, "There is something about a child's ability to find friendship and adventure in their own private universe with other children which is so true and so heartbreaking and ultimately gives us hope. And that is the core value that spoke to me in the book."

With the film in mid-development, Horberg joined Sidney Kimmel Entertainment (SKE), and Sidney Kimmel, in turn, became an enthusiastic supporter of the project. Jeff Skoll of Participant Productions was another early and passionate fan of the book, and joined with SKE as co-financiers.

In the midst of all this, the book burst onto bookstore shelves with an unexpected force, turning the novel into a cultural phenomenon. The filmmakers were at once astonished and thrilled at its sweeping popularity.

The Script

Once the rights were secured, the producers hired screenwriter David Benioff to transform the book into an epic, cinematic experience. "I always saw this as a story about cowardice and courage, and the journey between them," says Benioff. "And I wanted to make sure it remained a

Above: Director Marc Forster on horseback at Lake Caracol.

story of Afghanistan, of Afghans, of a people enduring the worst possible times, endless wars, and poverty— yet within that national horror, still finding the possibility of grace, beauty, and love."

One of the biggest challenges for Benioff was simply carving the sweeping, three-decade-long events of Amir's story into a two-hour motion picture. "Time jumps are difficult to navigate in a movie," explains the screenwriter. "The novel shows Amir at many different ages, but I decided early on that I wanted only two actors playing the role. Any more than that and I think you might lose the connection to this wonderful character. So the screenplay streamlines the novel's narrative. Luckily, the heart of Khaled's story is so strong I believe it maintains its power even within the restrictions of the screenplay format."

As for finding a director, the producers chose Marc Forster, largely because of the lyricism and humanity he brought to every film he has made, no matter the genre, ranging from the powerful emotions of *Monster's Ball* to the enchantment of *Finding Neverland* to the inventive comedy of *Stranger Than Fiction*. For Forster, the story was irresistible. "Reading the book was such an emotional and beautiful experience that I knew right away I wanted to be involved," he says. "For me, the challenge would be creating this incredibly epic journey while bringing the audience inside a very intimate story about a few individuals and the profound effect they have on each other's lives."

The Language Barrier

While David Benioff was still writing the screenplay, one of the film's most daring creative decisions was made: to shoot the film in the Dari language, one of two main tongues spoken in Afghanistan. "I felt that shooting the film in any other language other than Dari would be a mistake," claims Forster. "If you have kids in 1970s Afghanistan speaking

English, it just would not be right. You need that emotional connection to something real."

Benioff and Forster had extensive discussions about which lines in the film should be spoken in Dari and which in English. Then, when the intricate translations of Benioff's screenplay were completed, they sent the script back to Khaled Hosseini, who lent his own poetic ear to the tweaking of particular lines and the adding of various phrases. The result was a screenplay that is, according to Hosseini, "credible and beautiful Dari." (There are also a few lines in Pashto, a language spoken by the Taliban, and the Pakistani language, Urdu.)

To keep the language faithful to the material once production began, the filmmakers hired a team of native Dari speakers to coach the non-native actors on pronunciation and inflection. The production also hired several cultural advisors to validate the most nuanced details of the film's production. Scores of researchers were also consulted to ensure the verisimilitude of the film's content and representations.

Casting the Kids

Marc Forster was determined to cast the book's beloved characters with as much realism and integrity as possible, especially for young Amir and Hassan. Forster knew he needed two extraordinary young actors who could understand Amir and Hassan's cultural background, yet who would also breathe life into their boyish dreams and camaraderie and draw the audience into their innocent world of kites, fairy tales, and slingshot heroics. To find this daunting mix of qualities somewhere on earth, Forster recruited the London-based casting agent Kate Dowd.

Dowd's hunt began in the Afghan communities of Europe, the U.S., and Canada, with extensive open calls in London, Birmingham, Hamburg, Amsterdam, Toronto, New York, San Francisco, and Virginia. While many of the boys who auditioned could speak some Dari, their speech was already inflected with the regional accents of wherever they now lived. "Out of their dear little mouths came the accents of England or the U.S.," recalls Dowd, "and it just wasn't the right sound. That's when we realized

Above: Child actor Zekiria Ebrahimi (left) with director Marc Forster and fellow actor Ahmad Khan Mahmoodzada.

we had to go to Kabul to find our boys and much of the cast as well. We were not going to find them anywhere else!"

So Dowd wound up on an odyssey literally to the other side of the globe, to search for, in the words of producer Rebecca Yeldham, "eyes of wonder and sparkle." For an entire month, Dowd canvassed schools, orphanages, and even the playgrounds of bomb-shattered Kabul. She met one extraordinary, persevering child after another, and began shipping footage of the boys back to the U.S. Dowd weeded down her list of candidates to a promising group of remarkable children, and then invited Forster, already on his way to Kabul, to make the final decision.

Rather than hold formal auditions, Forster brought the local Afghan children outside to fly kites, to see them in a relaxed, playful, outgoing state of mind. Then he made his final casting decisions. Zekiria Ebrahimi, a fifth-grader whom Dowd uncovered in the local French Lycée, would play Amir. Ahmad Khan Mahmoodzada and Ali Danish Bakhtyari, who were both found through ARO, the Afghan Relief Organization, would play Hassan and Sohrab.

As Amir, young Zekiria would have to traverse a lot of difficult emotions, yet despite his lack of acting experience, he was a natural. "When I first met Zekiria, he was very shy and didn't say much," recalls Forster. "But there was something in his demeanor that was intriguing to me, a bit of a sadness somewhere. His father was killed before he was born, and his mother abandoned him. And it was because of this inherent sadness that I felt he would be the right choice to play young Amir, who lost his mother and felt his father didn't love him."

Forster was equally compelled by the personalities of Ahmad Khan Mahmoodzada, who so movingly brings to life the spirit and resilience of Hassan, even in the face of his unjust fate; and of Ali Danish as Hassan's son, Sohrab. "Ahmad had an unbelievable spirit of life, a fighting spirit of sorts," says Forster. "He had energy and vitality and conveyed a sense of not being afraid of anything, of being willing to take a big bite out of life, which was so important for portraying Hassan. And Ali Danish made me very emotional just looking at him. He has an incredible warmth and beauty and yet there is a distance you feel with him, an emotional wall, which is shared by Sohrab."

To gain permission to release the children from school and to wrangle travel passports for them, extensive negotiations over endless cups of tea and paperwork were required. "After Marc made his casting selections in Kabul, it took us three months just to process the cast!" recalls producer/unit production manager E. Bennett Walsh. "No one had birth certificates or ID cards, so we found ourselves in multiple meetings with government departments to get permission for issuing their passports." With assistance from many people and agencies across Afghan society as well as through circuitous diplomatic and ministerial channels, everything finally came together.

While in Kabul, Nabi Tanha was cast in the role of Ali, who is both Baba's servant and Hassan's father. The veteran Afghan actors Abdul Qadir Farookh and Maimoona Ghizal also joined the cast as General

Right: Ahmad Khan Mahmoodzada (Hassan) with Homayoun Ershadi, who plays Baba, Amir's father (and Hassan's real father, too).

Taheri and Jamilla, the San Francisco–based parents of Hassan's wife, Soraya. Abdul Salam Yusoufzai, an electrical engineer and furniture maker who has dabbled in the Afghan film industry, was cast as the adult Assef. In addition, numerous amateur Afghans, most of whom had never acted before, were cast in supporting roles. "In the end about 75 percent of the actors in the film came from Kabul," says Dowd.

Casting the Adults

Of course, the most important part of all was that of the adult Amir. To play this central role the filmmakers chose Khalid Abdalla, the 25-year-old actor of Egyptian ancestry who made an auspicious debut in *United 93* as the hijacker Ziad Jarrah.

For his part, Abdalla was deeply drawn to this complex character. "I believe the burden Amir carries is on account of his love," he says. "He did

something that's inexcusable, and some will blame him, but he was just a kid, and I think the guilt he carries suggests that his sense of things is right. To me his personal journey to confront his past and live up to what his father wanted from him, and to live up to all that Rahim Khan hoped for from him, is a very courageous one."

Prior to filming, Abdalla had never spoken a word of Dari, but he would have to speak both fluent Dari and English in the film, so he spent an entire month living in Kabul learning the language. He toured the city every day, soaking up the culture, and even receiving lessons in Afghan kite flying. "When I was in Kabul I let the novel be my tour guide," recalls Abdalla. "I went through the book and sought out every single detail of place, culture, or food in Kabul and then went see what all these things looked like, tasted like, or felt like."

Much of Amir's psyche has been formed in the shadow of his proud, strong-willed, academic father,

Baba. To play the role, the filmmakers chose Iranian actor Homayoun Ershadi, who was educated in architecture at the University of Venice but presently lives in Tehran. Of his character's transformation over the years, Ershadi says, "Baba is a very strong man but the problem with Baba is he doesn't see himself in his son Amir. He sees himself more in Hassan. He loves both of them and wants to see himself in Amir but he doesn't so it makes him angry. In the end, everything has changed and Baba no longer needs to see himself in Amir. He's a real father who shows his love."

Khaled Hosseini was won over by Ershadi's portrayal. "In the novel, Baba is this 6'5" guy who wrestles bears and he's this big, larger-than-life character and Homayoun is not that," he notes. "But he still conveys that gravitas, that sense of strength and presence. And when you see him scold Amir on the screen, you get the sense that this is truly somebody to be reckoned with."

Meanwhile, to play Baba's judicious friend, Rahim Kahn, the filmmakers turned to Shaun Toub, who gave a riveting performance as Farad in the Oscar®-winning *Crash*. "The first time I saw Shaun Toub in person, I instantly thought of him as Rahim Khan," says Forster. "He has that mix of calmness, wisdom, and kindness."

Also joining the cast was Atossa Leoni, an actress of Afghan and Iranian descent, in the role of Soraya, Amir's supportive wife. "Soraya is a very honest character," says Marc Forster, "and for me Atossa embodies that. She reveals a woman of many different layers: a traditional Afghan woman living in America, a portrait informed by being half Afghan and half Iranian herself, as well as someone with a wilder side. Not only did I feel all the turmoil in her character's life but also a genuine connection between her and Amir."

The actress was drawn to the character from the very start. "I really admire Soraya," says Leoni. "She's sensitive, vulnerable, and strong at the same time, and she's a very classic female character. She has that ability to put admiration onto her husband without losing herself at the same time."

Rounding out the main cast in the role of Farid is Saïd Taghmaoui, a

Above: (from left to right) Producer Rebecca Yeldham, Marc Forster, and Khalid Abdalla on set in China.

seasoned actor of Moroccan ancestry who lives in France. Forster had seen Taghmaoui in *La Haine* and *Three Kings*. "He has an incredible power and strength," says the director. "Saïd was a boxer and came from the street, lived on the street, and understands street life, which was key for Farid."

Taghmaoui loved the part his character plays in Amir's quest. "He's like a mirror to Amir," Taghmaoui comments. "Farid is very frank, very real, and very simple, and he tells the truth. It's difficult to hear the truth, especially when a guy like Amir is on his way to redemption. But when Farid brings Amir to see his old enemy Assef, he knows Amir has to face him alone to get back his respect and dignity and redeem himself."

When he saw the entire cast assembled on the set as the living, breathing characters who had for so long existed only in his imagination, Khaled Hosseini was astonished. "When I wrote the novel, I had a very clear mental image of what these characters looked like, how they walked, how they looked at you," Hosseini says. "But once I walked on the set, it was as if none of that existed. Suddenly my own mental image was supplanted and replaced by the faces, mannerisms, rhythm, and speech of these actors. That speaks volumes about their ability as performers."

Faraway Locations

From the very start, the question of where to shoot the film loomed over the production. The story required the wholesale re-creation of several disparate worlds that no longer exist, including the vibrant Kabul of the 1970s that was all but eradicated during the Soviet invasion and the Taliban-ravaged Kabul of 2000.

Where could the filmmakers possibly find the landscapes, architecture, and settings of 3,000-year-old Kabul, the utterly unique Silk Road frontier town, in a place that could also handle the logistical needs of a major film production? E. Bennett Walsh spent months exploring some 20 potential countries, but the surprise answer ultimately turned out to be in far-flung Central Asia, in the vast, sparsely populated Xinjiang Province of Western China.

Walsh's location photographs revealed a majestic and haunting desert

landscape between the ancient cities of Kashgar and Tashkurgan, starkly reminiscent of Afghanistan, which not coincidentally, it borders. Today, this remote section of the fabled Silk Road (once the link between the Roman and Chinese Empires) is a vibrant Islamic center within Chinese society, where Indian and Persian influences abound. In the desert oasis city of Kashgar, a melting pot of cultures and colorful bazaars lends magic to a terrain that varies from the arid moonscapes of the Taklimakan Desert (which ominously means "enter and never leave") to the surrounding, dizzyingly high mountain ranges.

Clearly, bringing a feature film production to this remote area was challenging. "Once we decided on China, there was an enormous amount of scouting and location work to come up with a plan," says Walter F. Parkes. "I don't think I've been to a place that felt more foreign. There were moments, particularly when we would visit markets outside the main city, that you honestly felt you stepped into the eighteenth century."

Old Town Kashgar would eventually serve as the prime location for

Scouting locations in Tashkurgan (from left): Akemusulitan Sulaimanxia, background casting; Mamat Imin, Xinjiang set decorator; Bennett Walsh, producer; Huang Fan, China production supervisor; Walter Parkes, producer; Carlos Conti, production designer; Marc Forster, director; Akbar Yiming, Xinjiang production manager; and Bill Horberg, producer.

most of the scenes of Kabul in the 1970s and in the year 2000, while the side streets across from the impressive and massive Id Kah Mosque stood in for Pakistani streets in Peshawar, including Rahim Khan's tea house. Constructed in 1442, the mosque is one of the largest in China, able to accommodate 10,000 worshippers.

For the dangerous escape of Baba and the young Amir from Afghanistan to Pakistan, as well as Amir's journey back again decades later with Farid to rescue Sohrab, the production shot on locations along the famed Karakoram Highway, the highest paved road in the world, which weaves precariously through some of the most breathtaking mountain passes in the world. Additional scenes were shot at Karakul Lake at 13,000 feet of elevation, where cast and crew were housed in yurts, the typical tent-like homes of that area.

The smaller city of Tashkurgan, known as "the Stone City" for its 2,000-year-old ruins, became the setting for additional street scenes of Kabul in the 1970s, as well as the haunting Kabul Cemetery, which Amir visits on his return. In addition, the production filmed for two weeks in Beijing. Three hours outside of Beijing, the production shot the terrifying scene of a Taliban stoning at the Baoding Stadium with 1,000 extras filling the seats. After shooting nearly three months in China, the production moved on to San Francisco, where they filmed the kite-flying scenes that bookend the film at Berkeley's Cesar Chavez Marina Park.

With over 28 countries represented on the cast and crew, the languages spoken on the set spanned from English (from the U.S., U.K., Australia, New Zealand, and South Africa) to Dari and Pashto, Farsi (from Iran), Urdu (from Pakistan), Uighur (from Xinjiang Province), Tajik (Tashkurgan), and Mandarin and Cantonese Chinese, in addition to German, Spanish, French, and Italian. It was sometimes only through charades that communication and collaboration somehow kept flowing.

"It did provide great humor at times," notes Rebecca Yeldham, "as you witnessed a Swiss director communicating to an Afghan Dari interpreter as well as to his 1st AD who is American and to a Chinese AD who speaks Mandarin, who is communicating to an AD who is speaking Uighur, who is communicating to extras who maybe only speak Tajik!"

Costume designer Frank Fleming, who worked with Marc Forster on Monster's Ball, Stay, and Stranger Than Fiction, was charged with creating a wardrobe for both the affluent life in 1970s Afghanistan and the terrorized Taliban-controlled country of the early 2000s. The snowsuit worn by young Amir (left) is shown in an early drawing (below.) The other costume drawings are for Saifo, the kite shop keeper (see page 59), Ali (Hassan's father), and Baba (Amir's father.) Right: Production design by Carlos Conti (graphic illustration by Maud Gircourt) of the scene where Amir convinces Hassan to slingshot a dog with a walnut.

Design

The full power of *The Kite Runner* is brought to life not only through the performances but also via the painstaking design of the film and the collective vision of director of photography Roberto Schaefer, costume designer Frank Fleming, and production designer Carlos Conti.

The considerable task of re-creating two Kabuls—one a burgeoning, colorful city in the 1970s and the other a shattered place of fear and oppression in 2000—in the Western Chinese boomtown of Kashgar fell to production designer Carlos Conti. "Carlos and I began by looking at images and reference pictures of Kabul and Peshawar," explains Forster, "and by the time we came to China, we had a very clear vision of what we wanted. We developed the idea of using contrasting colors to make the 1970s as beautiful as possible and then by 2000, to make everything gray, draining the color out of it to reflect the starkness of the times."

Once in Kashgar, one of Conti's biggest challenges was finding the right location for Baba's house, which represents the epitome of Kabul's

sophistication in its heyday. "We looked at a lot of photographs of homes in the once prestigious Wazir Akbar Khan District of Kabul, where Baba and Amir lived in the story," says Conti. "We then created our own house in the architectural style of Kabul in the 1970s but with the color schemes that we envisioned for the movie. We built the entire house in eight weeks on an empty lot that previously had donkeys, sheep, and chickens there. We built every piece of furniture and even created the paintings."

Another major location the production design team labored over was Kabul's Kite Square, in which the spectacular kite-fighting tournament turns all eyes to the sky for the suspenseful battles. The scene was shot in Kashgar's Ostangboye Square.

When Amir and Farid return to a very different Kabul, living under Taliban rule, Conti's idea was to contrast the bursting energy of children playing in the streets and vendors hawking their wares in the 1970s with an eerie,

pained silence and stark nothingness. "I discussed with Marc the idea of having very little in the frame and no cars in the scene when Amir and Farid return. That creates a strong impression of a time when no one was allowed to fly kites, play music, watch television, or go to the movies. It's an image that, in a few seconds, allows you to understand what happened in Afghanistan. My goal was to work in these simple, strong images throughout the design," he explains.

Also contributing to the naturalistic look of the film is the powerful work of director of photography Roberto Schaefer, who mixed the raw and the epic, relying largely on the existing lighting conditions available to him in Kashgar while at the same time filling the screen with awe-inspiring landscapes, textures, and colors. "The budget wasn't epic but Marc and I both thought this should still feel like an epic film," says Schaefer. "He wanted it to be as big and rich as possible, so I made the most out of everything that was available to us in order to show off the different periods, locations, and landscapes to give the film scale."

Shooting in the rugged deserts of Xianjiang posed numerous challenges, as the harsh reality behind the stunning vistas was often searing heat, lens-clouding dirt, and the occasional rogue dust storm. With his reliance on natural light, Schaefer also often found himself doing battle with the sun's ever-shifting directions, but he always found solutions.

"In telling the story of *The Kite Runner* we all went through our own emotional and personal journey," Marc Forster says, "that was filled with struggles and changes and realizations, and sometimes not knowing what was going to happen the next day. We got a glimpse of lives that are incredible, painful, and hard in an Afghanistan that has endured 30 years of war. But at the same time, we encountered so many people with extraordinary resilience. And that is what stays with you—that people always have this ability to rise above." ■

Left: Production design by Carlos Conti (with graphic illustration by Maud Gircourt) showing the scene where Baba proudly drives his new Mustang into the town square. Below left: Production designer Carlos Conti and producer Bill Horberg. Below: Child actor Zekiria Ebrahimi with director of photography Roberto Schaefer on location in China.

The Kite Runner
Shooting Script

Soraya   Amir

EXT. LAKE ELIZABETH PARK – DAY

TITLE CARD:

San Francisco, California, 2000

We trail a five-year-old BOY as he runs toward Lake Elizabeth.

Amir (34) stands by the lake, watching the water. He has a certain elegance, a professorial demeanor heightened by the smattering of gray in his thick, dark hair.

Amir sees his wife, Soraya, kiss a FRIEND good-bye and walk his way. Her thick black eyebrows are like the arched wings of a flying bird.

Amir wraps his arm around her. Alone together, they walk away from the park, away from the laughing children.

EXT. AMIR'S BUILDING – DAY

Two packages wait beneath the door. Amir picks them up.

> **SORAYA**
> Is that what I think it is?

> **AMIR**
> I think so.

Clearly this is a significant package and they're both excited, though perhaps Soraya's happiness is a bit more forced than Amir's.

> **SORAYA**
> Are you nervous?

> **AMIR**
> As long as they spelled my name right. . .

She unlocks the door and they enter.

INT. STUDY – DAY

Their home is small but tastefully decorated, with Persian rugs on the floor and tapestries hanging from the walls. Picture windows look out over Golden Gate Park.

Books are everywhere. Books crammed on the shelves, books stacked on stools, books in great piles beside the armchair.

Amir sets the package on his desk and opens it with a pen.

> **SORAYA**
> *(teasing)*
> You want a moment alone with it?

> **AMIR**
> I want you right here with me.

The box is filled with hardcover novels.

> **AMIR**
> There it is.

> **SORAYA**
> There it is.

He pulls one out and proudly inspects it.

Soraya stands beside her husband and looks over his shoulder.

> **SORAYA**
> Your baby.

Amir glances at her and we get a sense of tension between them, but Amir defuses the moment by kissing her on the forehead. The phone rings.

> **AMIR**
> I'll get it.

He walks out of the study, leaving his wife to consider his book.

INT. LIVING ROOM – DAY

Amir walks into the room and picks the ringing phone up, placing his book down. *A Season for Ashes.*

> **AMIR**
> Hello?

For a moment there is no response, only the static wash of a bad connection.

> **AMIR**
> Hello?

> **RAHIM KHAN (O.S.)**
> Amir jan.

It takes him a second to place the voice.

> **AMIR**
> Rahim Khan?

> **RAHIM KHAN (O.S.)**
> It is kind of you to remember.

INT. BATHROOM – DAY

Soraya walks in and sets the bath water running.

Soraya is a thousand miles away from the tastefully tiled bathroom.

INT. LIVING ROOM – DAY

Amir holds the phone to his ear, gazing out his window.

> **RAHIM KHAN**
> I've missed you, Amir jan.

Amir smiles to himself.

> **AMIR**
> It's good to hear your voice.

> **RAHIM KHAN (O.S.)**
> I've missed you, Amir jan. You should come home.

> **AMIR**
> *(raising his eyebrows)*
> Home? I don't know if now's such a great time.

> **RAHIM KHAN (O.S.)**
> It's a very bad time. But you should come.
> *(beat)*
> There is a way to be good again.

The words have an obvious effect on Amir. He stands very still, lips slightly parted, staring out the living room window.

Ext. Kabul – Day

The sky is blue and clear. A red kite duels a blue kite, spinning around each other, their glass strings glittering in the cold light.

TITLE CARD:
Kabul, Afghanistan, 1978

A horde of YOUNG BOYS stands in an empty lot on the city's outskirts, watching the kites battle.

One of the boys is the young AMIR (11), slender and awkward, a bit intimidated in the throng of boisterous, shoving boys.

> **OMAR**
> Take the spool. Hold it right.

Beside Amir stands HASSAN (10), a boy with a face like a Chinese doll. Hassan is an Hazara; his Mongol features set him apart from the other boys in the crowd, all Pashtuns.

Amir wears American-style blue jeans and a clean, new down parka. Hassan wears a bright green *chapan* (a traditional Afghan coat) over a thick sweater.

Unlike Amir, Hassan is not bothered by the roughhousing boys. If someone pushes him he pushes back, without malice or fear.

OMAR (14), an older boy with a wisp of mous-

Hassan

tache, controls his kite with great skill and confidence. He allows himself a small smile as he guides his kite into a superior position.

OMAR
Give me the string! Hold the spool right.

Hassan smiles as Omar's kite surges above the other, glass string cutting the adversary free from its line.

OMAR
I cut him! Victory!

The defeated kite slowly glides south. All the boys run in that direction, hollering and elbowing each other.

Hassan takes off in the other direction. Amir stares at him.

HASSAN
This way!

Hassan whirls around, motioning with his hand.

AMIR
Where are you going?

Amir looks at the kite, drifting steadily south. He looks at Hassan, sprinting north again. Finally Amir chases after him.

Though Amir is a bit older and taller, Hassan is the natural athlete.

EXT. KABUL – NARROW STREET – DAY

They run through the ancient streets of Kabul, hopping gutters, weaving through narrow alleys.

EXT. KABUL – ANIMAL MARKET – DAY

Amir can't keep pace with the faster boy. He looks up again. The kite is nowhere to be seen.

AMIR
We're losing it!

Hassan, far ahead, doesn't even bother looking for the kite.

HASSAN
Trust me!

Amir hobbles after him.

EXT. Kabul – Dirt Road – Day

He turns the corner and finds himself on a rutted dirt road. Hassan sits cross-legged in the dirt, eating from a fistful of dried mulberries.

AMIR
What are we doing here?

HASSAN
Sit with me, Amir agha.

Production design by Carlos Conti; graphic illustration by Maud Gircourt.

Amir drops next to him, wheezing from their run.

AMIR
You're wasting time here. The kite went the other way.

Hassan pops a mulberry in his mouth. He's not winded at all.

HASSAN
It will come this way.

AMIR
How do you know?

HASSAN
I know.

AMIR
But, how?

HASSAN
Have I ever lied to you?

AMIR
How should I know?

HASSAN
  (indignant)
I'd rather eat dirt.

AMIR
  (testing)
Would you really do that?

HASSAN
  (puzzled)
Do what?

AMIR
Eat dirt if I told you to.

Hassan searches Amir's face, trying to decide if his playmate is joking or not. When Hassan speaks he is completely serious, staring into the older boy's eyes.

HASSAN
If you asked, I would.

Hassan cannot hold the boy's gaze. He looks away.

HASSAN
But would you really ask me to do such a thing?

AMIR
Are you crazy? You know I wouldn't.

Hassan looks to the sky.

HASSAN
I know.

Hassan stands and walks a few paces to his left. Amir looks up. He watches in awe as the red kite plummets towards them.

Amir hears footfalls and shouts; he turns and sees the approaching kite runners—the boys they stood with before.

But they're wasting their time. Hassan stands with his arms wide open, smiling, as the kite drops right into his hands.

INT. LIVING ROOM – DAY

A hand writes a check on a magnificent antique desk.

An OLDER MAN wearing a cheap gray suit stands in front of the desk, hands clasped, watching nervously.

The hands belong to BABA, a towering Pashtun with a thick beard and curly brown hair. His hands look capable of uprooting a willow tree as he hands the man the check.

> **OLDER MAN**
> Thank you, Agha sahib.

Rahim Khan sits beside Baba. He lacks his old friend's charisma and physical presence, but his kind eyes and wry smile make him more approachable.

> **BABA**
> I want them to start building tomorrow.
> This should have happened a long time ago.

ALI, a servant with a slight limp, refills the men's cups of tea. Baba accepts his with a smile. He and Ali have known each other their whole lives; there should be a sense of easy rapport between them. Ali leaves.

When Baba finishes with the papers he stands and hands them across the desk to the older man, who glances at the papers and holds them carefully, as if they were something precious.

The older man nods vigorously as he leaves.

> **OLDER MAN**
> Absolutely, Sahib. And thank you! The orphans of Kabul will never forget you.

Baba turns to Rahim Khan contemplatively.

> **BABA**
> Somehow. . . I suspect they will.

Rahim Khan leans forward to Baba, who calmly sips his tea.

> **RAHIM KHAN**
> You know the bureaucrats will steal half the money.

Baba

Rahim Kahn

BABA

Only half? They've gotten lazy.

A beat of dismay and Rahim Khan shares the small laugh.

EXT. WAZIR AKBAR KHAN DISTRICT – DUSK

Amir and Hassan walk across a small wooden bridge, singing a song. Amir now carries the kite.

AMIR

Hey Mister Jaylawni/conjure up the winds for me.

HASSAN

Hey Mister Jaylawni/conjure up the winds for me.

HASSAN

You could have beaten him.

Amir gives Hassan a doubtful look.

AMIR

Me? Weren't you watching Omar back there? He never loses.

HASSAN

If you have the right kite, you'll win the tournament this year.

INT. BABA'S HOUSE - LATER

Baba sorts papers as he listens to a radio program.

RADIO ANNOUNCER

With the victory of Saur Revolution, for the first time in the history of this century. . .

EXT. BABA'S HOUSE – LATER

The boys walk up a brick driveway lined with poplar trees. Baba's house is the most beautiful in the district. A broad entryway flanked by rose-bushes leads to the sprawling manse.

RADIO ANNOUNCER (O.S.)

. . . the political sovereignty and political power have been bestowed upon the Democratic Party of the People of Afghanistan.

Hassan hurries ahead. On the south end of the garden, in the shadows of a loquat tree, stands a little mud hut: the servants' home.

The door of the hut is open. Amir watches Hassan step inside and greet his father, ALI.

Amir walks into his imposing home.

INT. BABA'S HOUSE – CONTINUOUS

Gold-stitched tapestries line the walls.

The radio plays a speech delivered by a MARXIST IDEOLOGUE. We only pick up fragments but these are ominous:

MARXIST IDEOLOGUE (O.S.)

The imperialists will lose because they sneer at history, because they sneer at the workers, because they sneer at the people!
    (cheers from a crowd)
They can sit behind their high walls, they can drive their American cars, but once the hunt begins, they will never stop running!

Rahim Khan reads the newspaper as Baba sorts his files.

RAHIM KHAN

This will get bloody before it gets better.

BABA

Usually a safe bet.

Unseen in the adjacent foyer, Amir enters the front door, kite in hand.

RAHIM KHAN

They say the Communists are starting brawls at the University. A student was stabbed last week.

Amir sneaks through the foyer and up the stairs, avoiding the adult voices. He hasn't been noticed.

RAHIM KHAN

I'm glad Amir's too young to be involved in all this.

BABA
Amir?
(*snorts*)
Trust me, he won't be getting into any brawls.

At the sound of his name, Amir pauses on the steps.

BABA
Sometimes I see him playing on the street with the neighborhood boys. They push him around, take his toys from him. But Amir. . . he never fights back. Never.

Amir eavesdrops from the stairs, troubled by his father's words.

RAHIM KHAN
So he's not violent.

BABA
You know what happens when the other kids tease him? Hassan steps in and fends them off. I've seen it with my own eyes. And when they come home, I say to him, "How did Hassan get that scrape on his face" and he says, "He fell down."
(*beat*)
There's something missing in that boy.

Baba lights a cigarette and Rahim Khan sighs heavily, looking up from his paper.

RAHIM KHAN
My friend. . . children aren't coloring books. You don't get to fill them with your favorite colors.
(*beat*)
He's not like you. He'll never be like you. But watch. He'll turn out well.

BABA
A boy who won't stand up for himself becomes a man who won't stand up for anything.

Rahim Khan turns and looks through the open study door, perhaps hearing Amir climbing the stairs.

Int. Baba's House – Continuous

Amir goes to his bedroom, dragging the brightly colored kite on the floor behind him.

INT. AMIR'S ROOM – LATER

Amir sits at his desk, reading through a sheaf of handwritten pages. He doesn't answer when there's a knock on the door.

Amir looks up from his papers but says nothing. After a moment, Rahim Khan opens the door.

RAHIM KHAN
Amir jan. . . may I come in?

Amir doesn't respond, so Rahim Khan steps into the room.

RAHIM KHAN
I wanted to say goodbye. I'm leaving for Pakistan tomorrow.

Rahim Khan notices the red kite lying on the floor.

RAHIM KHAN
That's a fine kite.

AMIR
Hassan ran it down.

RAHIM KHAN
The boy's got a gift.

Amir nods, not keen to discuss Hassan's kite running.

RAHIM KHAN
What are you working on?

AMIR
A story.

A boy who won't stand up for himself becomes a man who won't stand up for anything.

RAHIM KHAN
May I read it?

AMIR
It's not very good.

RAHIM KHAN
All the same, I'd love to read it.

Amir stares at the story. Finally he hands it to Rahim Khan.

RAHIM KHAN
Thank you, Amir jan. I'll read it tonight.

He turns to leave.

AMIR
He hates me because I killed her.

Rahim Khan turns and stares at Amir, not comprehending.

AMIR
My mother.

Rahim Khan speaks to the back of Amir, who stairs straight into his reflection in the window.

RAHIM KHAN
Amir. . . don't ever say such a thing. Don't ever think it.

AMIR
But it's true.

Rahim crouches beside the boy's chair.

RAHIM KHAN
It's a dangerous thing, being born. Dangerous for the mother, dangerous for the child.
(beat)
Your father would die for you. You know that, don't you?

Amir shrugs and says nothing. Rahim Khan gives him a sad smile, puts his hand on the boy's head.

RAHIM KHAN
Amir jan.

Ext. Wazir Akbar Khan District - Day

Amir and Hassan sit on a wall overlooking the neighborhood. They play cards and crack walnuts in their palms to eat.

AMIR
Come on, do it.

HASSAN
It's wrong, Amir agha.

AMIR
Do you have to be so holy all the time?

Hassan sighs.

HASSAN
Just one?

AMIR
Just one.

He and Amir look toward the neighbor's yard, where an overweight German Shepherd sleeps by the porch.

Hassan picks up an old, flimsy slingshot, loads a whole walnut into it and takes aim.

The walnut hisses through the air and hits the sleeping dog in his haunch. The dog leaps to his feet, whimpering as it runs away.

AMIR
You think one day he'd wise up.

He pulls a smooth, folded Afghani bill from his pocket.

HASSAN
You got your allowance?

Amir pulls the bill taut between his fingers.

AMIR
Yeah, how about we see *The Magnificent Seven* again?

Hassan's face lights up. The boys hop down from the wall and chase each other across the yard, making guns from their fingers and thumbs, firing make-believe bullets.

> ### AMIR
> *(affecting a macho accent)*
> We deal in lead, friend.

INT. CINEMA ZAINAB – DAY

The Magnificent Seven plays on the screen. Charles Bronson and Yul Brynner confer in dubbed Farsi.

> ### YUL BRYNNER
> I'm a friend of Harry Luck's. He tells me you're broke.
>
> ### CHARLES BRONSON
> No. I'm doing this because I'm an eccentric millionaire.
>
> ### YUL BRYNNER
> There's a job for six men, watching over a village south of the border.

In the crowd, Amir and Hassan's faces are illuminated by the flickering images.

I admire your notion

of fair odds, mister.

CHARLES BRONSON
How big's the opposition?

YUL BRYNNER
Thirty guns.

HASSAN
I admire your notion of fair odds, mister.

AMIR
I admire your notion of fair odds, mister.

CHARLES BRONSON
I admire your notion of fair odds, mister.

The boys' faces alight with smiles.

YUL BRYNNER
Harry tells me you faced bigger odds in the Travis County War.

Ext. Wazir Akbar Khan District - Day

Amir and Hassan walk through the streets, humming the Elmer Bernstein score from *The Magnificent Seven*.

HASSAN
Who's your favorite?

AMIR
Steve McQueen.

HASSAN
I like Charles Bronson.
(beat)
Maybe someday we'll go to Iran.

Amir squints at Hassan in confusion.

AMIR
Why?

HASSAN
Maybe we'd see him somewhere. I could get his autograph.

AMIR
Charles Bronson's not Iranian.

HASSAN
He's not?
(contemplative beat)
So why does he speak Farsi with an Iranian accent?

A rock strikes Amir in the back. The boys whirl around. ASSEF (15) strolls toward them, flanked by his entourage, WALI (14) and KAMAL (14). All three wear jeans and T-shirts.

ASSEF
Where are you going, faggots?

Amir turns around nervously. Already broad-shouldered and deep-voiced, Assef towers over the other kids.

ASSEF
(to Wali and Kamal)
What do you boys think: if I paid you to be my friends, would you really be my friends? Or would you be my servants?

WALI
Gee Assef, if you were paying us, we'd be your servants.

ASSEF
So I guess Amir has no friends.

AMIR
(voice trembling)
We're not bothering you.

ASSEF
Wrong. You are bothering me. Afghanistan's the land of the Pashtuns. We're the true Afghans, not this Flat-Nose Hazara. His people pollute our homeland. They dirty our blood. If idiots like you and your father didn't take these people in, we'd be rid of them.

Wali and Kamal nod. Assef advances on Amir, grinning. Amir cowers, too frightened even to run. But a screeching car distracts Assef.

> **HASSAN (O.S.)**
> Please leave us alone, Agha.

Assef turns. Hassan holds the slingshot in his hands, the elastic band pulled all the way back. The stone sits in the cup, aimed at Assef's face.

Assef's eyes widen with surprise. Wali and Kamal look even more astonished. Hassan's hand trembles with the strain of the taut elastic band.

ASSEF
Put it down, you motherless Hazara.

HASSAN
Please leave us in peace.

ASSEF
Maybe you didn't notice, but there are three of us and two of you.

HASSAN
And maybe you didn't notice that I'm the one holding the slingshot.

Assef looks from the rock to Hassan. He searches

the boy's face, trying to gauge his resolve.

ASSEF
Forget it.

Assef turns and walks away, followed by his two henchmen.

ASSEF
We'll deal with these faggots later.

Amir and Hassan watch them go. When Amir finally turns to Hassan, the smaller boy eases his slingshot down with trembling hands.

Int. Baba's House, Dining Room – Morning

Amir sits at the dining room table, hastily finishing his homework.

Hassan hands him an envelope.

AMIR
What's this?

HASSAN
Rahim Khan left it for you.

Amir tears open the envelope. He reads the letter quickly, a broad smile spreading across his face.

AMIR
He liked it!

HASSAN
Liked what?

AMIR
My story!

HASSAN
Well of course he liked it, Amir agha. You tell great stories.

AMIR
"*Bravo*," he wrote. Bravo!

HASSAN
Bravo!

AMIR
Do you know what "bravo" means?

HASSAN
No.

AMIR
It's Italian for genius.

HASSAN
What's the story about?

Amir puts the letter aside, content with his new-found literary fame.

AMIR
It's about a man who finds a magic cup. And he learns that if he weeps into the cup, his tears turn to pearls. He's very poor, you know. And at the end of the story, he's sitting on a mountain of pearls with a bloody knife in his hand and his dead wife in his arms.

Hassan frowns, confused for a moment.

HASSAN
So he killed her. . .

AMIR
Yes, Hassan.

HASSAN
So that he'd cry and get rich!

AMIR
Yes. You're very quick.

Hassan nods, and turns away.

AMIR
What?

HASSAN
Nothing, Amir agha. Are you done with breakfast?

Hassan clears the dirty plate and cup.

AMIR
What?

HASSAN
Well. . . will you permit me to ask a question about the story?

AMIR
Of course.

HASSAN
Why did the man have to kill his wife?

AMIR
Because each of his tears becomes a pearl!

HASSAN
Yes, but why couldn't he just smell an onion?

Amir opens his mouth to berate the boy but then realizes that Hassan has a point.

Ext. Baba's House - Day

Hassan repairs some broken wire on a pigeon cage.

INT. STUDY – EVENING

Amir sits at a desk, watching Hassan work outside. Baba stands by the wet bar in the corner of the room, pouring himself a whiskey.

AMIR
The mullahs at school say drinking is a sin. They say drinkers will pay when the Reckoning comes.

Baba walks behind him and swallows some whiskey.

BABA
Do you want to know what your father thinks about sin?

AMIR
Yes.

BABA
Then I'll tell you. But first understand this and understand it now: You'll never learn anything of value from those bearded idiots.

AMIR
You mean the mullahs?

BABA
I piss on the beards of those self-righteous monkeys.

Amir seems shocked to hear such blasphemy.

BABA
They do nothing but thumb their prayer beads and recite a book written in a tongue they don't even understand.
(beat)
There is only one sin. And that is theft. Every other sin is a variation of theft. Do you understand that?

EXT. BABA'S HOUSE – CONTINUOUS

Hassan chases the pigeons, which have gotten loose.

INT. STUDY – CONTINUOUS

Air watches Hassan's attempts to catch the birds.

AMIR
No, Baba jan.

Baba takes a seat behind his son.

BABA
When you kill a man, you steal a life. You steal his wife's right to her husband, his children's right to a father.

But Amir is intently focused on Hassan putting pigeons back in their cages outside.

BABA
There is no act more wretched than stealing. Do you see?

AMIR
Yes, Baba.

BABA
Good.

Baba drains the last of his whiskey with a single swallow. He stands and returns to the bar.

BABA
All this talk of sinning is making me thirsty.

Int. Servant's Hut - Day

Hassan and his father, Ali, kneel on the prayer rugs, intone the prayers, and bow their heads to the ground three times.

AMIR (O.S.)
Hassan! Hassan!

ALI
Go, he's calling you.

Hassan stands and Hassan runs outside.

EXT. BABA'S HOUSE – CONTINUOUS

Amir stands by the reflective pool, waiting for Hassan.

AMIR
Happy birthday.

He hands a clumsily wrapped gift to Hassan, who grins and tears it open. Inside is a brand-

new Fly Bye slingshot.

AMIR
It's made in America.

Hassan cradles the slingshot in his palms like a newborn infant. He smiles at Amir, his eyes wet with happiness.

AMIR
I figured, if you're going to be my body-guard, you need a proper weapon.

HASSAN
Thank you, Amir agha.

AMIR
Come on, let's go.

EXT. CEMETERY – DAY

An abandoned cemetery sprawls across the hill-top. Tangles of brushwood clog aisles of un-marked headstones. A pomegranate tree rises near the rusty iron gate.

Hassan sits beside the tree, scooping the bloody seeds from the fruit, wiping his hands on the grass.

Amir uses a pocketknife to carve words into the bark of the tree. When he finishes, Hassan runs his fingers over the letters.

HASSAN

What does it say?

AMIR

Amir and Hassan, the Sultans of Kabul.

HASSAN

The Sultans of Kabul!

Amir sits again and pulls a leather-bound book, the Shahnamah, from his satchel.

AMIR

You want a story?

HASSAN

Rostam and Sohrab!

AMIR

Not them again. I've read you that one fifty times. How about Rudabeh?

HASSAN

It's your book, Amir agha.

Amir sees Hassan's disappointment.

AMIR

All right, all right. Rostam and Sohrab. It's your birthday.

Hassan grins and sits next to him, looking over his shoulder as Amir flips to the proper page and begins to read.

AMIR

Give ear unto the combat of Sohrab against Rostam, though it be a tale replete with tears. . .

EXT. CEMETERY – LATER

A loud honking interrupts the reading. The boys turn and run down to see a gleaming, black '68 Ford Mustang pull up at the bottom of the hill. Baba sits in the driver's seat.

HASSAN

Your dad got a new car?

Amir shoves the book into the satchel and the two boys sprint down to the Mustang, Hassan getting there far quicker.

HASSAN

Isn't this the car they drive in *Bullitt*?

Baba honks again as the boys reach the car.

HASSAN

It's Steve McQueen! It's Steve McQueen!

BABA

I heard it was someone's birthday.

Hassan climbs into the cramped backseat.

BABA

It's your day, Hassan. Why don't you sit up front?

Hassan glances at Amir, who reluctantly switches seats. Baba smiles at Hassan. He seems warmer and more comfortable with the Hazara boy than he is with his own son.

BABA

Are you ready for your birthday present?

HASSAN

Is it a drawing book?

BABA

Better.

HASSAN

A toy gun?

Baba shifts into drive.

The Sultans of Kabul!

BABA
Better.

The Mustang's rear tires kick up cattails of gravel and dust. Hassan has a giant smile as they speed away.

EXT. JADEH MAYWAND – DAY

Baba, Amir and Hassan drive down the crowded street south of the Kabul River. Street vendors hawk lamb kebabs and dates; merchants sell everything from fresh fish to ornate rugs.

A few American hippies, their hair long and unwashed, wearing bead necklaces and sandals, stroll through the marketplace.

The Mustang pulls up to a store no larger than a prison cell and they pile out.

BABA
Uncle Saifo!

SAIFO, a nearly-blind old man, greets them as they enter his shop.

SAIFO
My brother! It's been too long. Everyone good?

Int. Saifo's – Day

SAIFO leads the boys through his shop to a hidden room in the back.

BABA
It's his birthday, he can have any kite he wants.

Here, Saifo's true art is revealed. Dozens of colorful kites hang from the walls and ceiling.

SAIFO
Here they are. Take your pick.

Saifo's kites are masterpieces, the paper wings cut to perfect proportions, the frames tight and true.

Amir and Hassan examine the wares with expert eyes and fingers, trying to determine which kites would have the best loft, which would be easiest to maneuver.

Hassan picks out a striking white kite with black, red and green designs.

HASSAN
I want that one.

BABA
(to Saifo)
We'll take it.

Hassan beams, proud of Baba's approval. Amir watches in silence from a corner of the shop.

BABA
A good choice.

INT. SHED – DAY

Amir and Hassan prepare the tar, the cutting line used to decapitate other kites, feeding hundreds of feet of string through a mixture of ground glass and glue.

AMIR
I was just lucky that time.

HASSAN
It wasn't luck, Amir Agha. You're better than him.

The section of the string already coated with glass hangs between two poles to dry.

HASSAN
I know you're going to win.

AMIR
You have too much faith in me.

EXT. BABA'S HOUSE – NIGHT

The first flakes of snow are starting to fall.

BABA (O.S.)
Ali made the cauliflower especially for you.

RAHIM KHAN
Yes. Every time I come he makes the cauliflower.

Through the dining room window, Ali can be seen serving curried cauliflower over rice.

BABA
I know. You come here too often.

Baba turns to Amir, sitting next to him.

BABA
The tournament's tomorrow. Are you and Hassan ready?

AMIR
We've been practicing.

BABA
Did I ever tell you about the year I won?

RAHIM KHAN
I'm fairly sure you told everyone in Kabul about the year you won.

INT. DINING ROOM – CONTINUOUS

Visible through the doorway, Hassan happily listens as he prepares the tea cups.

BABA
Fourteen kites I cut down. I think that's still a record.

RAHIM KHAN
Yes, yes, yes. Eat.

Ext. Wazir Akbar Khan District - Day

The sky is a blameless blue. Snow dusts the buildings throughout the block.

Children from all over Kabul crowd the rooftops. KITE FIGHTERS huddle with their SPOOL HOLDERS, talking last-minute tactics. At least fifty kites of all colors already hang in the sky, paper sharks roaming for prey.

Hassan walks down the center of the street. Amir runs out of Baba's house.

Hassan wears black rubber boots and a bright red chapan over a thick sweater and faded corduroy pants. Amir wears a khaki snow suit.

> **HASSAN**
> I think you're going to make Agha sahib very proud today.

> **AMIR**
> You think so?

> **HASSAN**
> *Inshallah.*

> **AMIR**
> (skeptical)
> *Inshallah.*

The streets are crowded with kite fighters and spectators.

Amir looks up to the balcony and sees Baba and Rahim Khan, both dressed in wool sweaters, sipping tea. Baba waves.

> **AMIR**
> It's really crowded.

Amir shifts his feet, staring at the crowds of kite fighters.

> **AMIR**
> I'm not sure it's the best day to fly a kite.

HASSAN
Why? It's a beautiful day.

The boys keep walking, Hassan smiling confident, Amir unsure.

HASSAN
It's the two of us against all of Kabul. And we're going to win.

AMIR
I admire your notion of fair odds, mister.

The two boys exchange a smile.

HASSAN
Let's fly.

He lifts the kite, white with red, black, and green.

He runs with the kite, the spool rolling in Amir's hands until Hassan stops, fifty feet away, and holds the kite over his head.

HASSAN
Put down the spool.
(Amir does)
Take it!

Hassan tosses the kite.

Amir pulls on the string, coaxing the kite into flight. Soon it soars above them, making a sound like a paper bird flapping its wings.

More and more kite fighters fill the streets, jerking and tugging on their lines, squinting up to the sky, trying to gain position to cut the opponent's line.

Every kite fighter has an assistant who holds the spool and feeds the glass line. Hassan spools for Amir.

HASSAN
Take it under!

The cutting begins and the first defeated kite whirls out of control.

AMIR
We cut him! We cut him!

HASSAN
We cut him! We cut him!

The kite runners pursue it, chasing the wind-blown kite as it drifts through the neighborhoods.

Hordes of runners go after each fallen kite, swarming the streets like the bull runners of Pamplona.

Kites fall from the sky like shooting stars with brilliant, rippling tails.

Hassan sees Omar, the talented kite fighter seen earlier, flying his brilliant blue kite at the end of the street.

From the balcony, Baba and Rahim Khan observe excitedly.

BABA
It's getting close. If he takes the last kite he's the winner.

Amir keeps stealing glances at Baba, on the edge of his seat.

HASSAN
Amir agha! Go a little to your right!

Amir returns his gaze to the sky just in time to see a green kite closing in on his own bird.

Amir plays with the wire, manipulating his kite into a complex dance. Amir comes out on top, his kite's glass wire slicing the green kite's string.

AMIR
We cut him! We cut him!

HASSAN
We cut him! We cut him!

The green kite plummets to earth as Amir and Hassan jump for joy and a band of yelling boys chases after it.

From the balcony Baba and Rahim Khan grow excited.

Amir agha! Go a little to your right!

RAHIM KHAN
They could break your record.

BABA
Let's see.

On another rooftop, Omar is cheered on by the crowd. He turns to his spooler.

OMAR
Hold the spool right.

CROWD
Take him, Omar!

The blue kite soars and spins, slicing a black kite free. His OPPONENT throws his string in frustration.

OMAR
I cut him! Victory! Victory!

Amir keeps his eye on Omar's blue kite, flying through the air with intimidating grace, its glass wire shimmering in the failing sunlight.

AMIR
How many has he cut?

HASSAN
I counted twelve.

AMIR
I think he wants Baba's record.

HASSAN
We can't let that happen.

Omar sets his sights on Amir and Hassan's kite.

OMAR'S SPOOLER
Last one, Omar agha.

The kites sweep and soar. Hassan looks on anxiously.

HASSAN
Pull your string forward!

Baba stands up in anticipation, sparking spectators on the streets and rooftops to stomp their feet, clapping, whistling, chanting:

SPECTATORS

Cut him! Cut him!

Amir's kite and the deadly blue kite are the final survivors. Amir sees the blue kite diving toward his kite, trying to take advantage of Amir's lack of altitude.

RAHIM KHAN

It's just the two of them now.

A chase begins, and it's a chase of two master kite fighters, their paper birds winging over the streets, trailed by their shadows on the snow.

The blue kite seems to sense its danger. It jerks up, down and sideways, trying desperately to escape. Amir's kite closes in relentlessly. The crowd knows the end is near.

Amir's kite whips past the blue kite, severing its line. The crowd roars.

Hassan howls with joy. He runs over to Amir and wraps his arm around the older boy's neck.

HASSAN

Bravo, Amir agha! You cut him. We won! We won!

Amir blinks. For a moment he can't move. Finally he whoops and throws his free arm around Hassan. The boys hop up and down, laughing so hard they're almost weeping.

Amir sees Baba standing on the edge of his rooftop, pumping both his fists, hollering at the top of his lungs. Rahim Khan stands beside Baba, grinning broadly.

Amir beams. He seems to grow as he basks in the light of his father's pride, standing taller, smiling more brightly.

HASSAN

Amir, I'm going to run that blue kite for you.

He hands him the spool and runs, the hem of his green *chapan* dragging in the snow behind him.

AMIR

Hassan! Come back with it!

Hassan stops and turns, cupping his hands around his mouth.

HASSAN

For you, a thousand times over!

He smiles and disappears as every kite runner on the streets, a band of forty shoving boys, takes off after it.

Amir begins to pull his kite in from the sky as people rush to congratulate him, lifting him on their shoulders.

Assef, Wali, and Kamal sit on a bench mocking the running children around them.

On the rooftop, Omar turns on his spooler, who offers him the remaining string.

> **OMAR**
> What am I supposed to do with this?
> You're the reason I got cut!

EXT. STREET – DUSK

The sun sinks behind the hills. The sky is painted pink and purple. A mullah bellows azan from the Haji Yaghoub Mosque.

The bazaar is emptying quickly. Amir picks his way through the dwindling crowd, past the LAME BEGGARS dressed in layers of tattered rags, past VENDORS with rugs on their shoulders, past BUTCHERS closing shop for the day.

He stops by a dried fruit stand. A MERCHANT wearing a blue turban loads his mule with crates of pine seeds and raisins.

> **AMIR**
> Have you seen a Hazara boy come this way? Wearing a red *chapan*?

> **MERCHANT**
> *(pointing south)*
> I saw a boy running that way. He had a kite in his hand.

The merchant grunts and ties another bag closed.

> **MERCHANT**
> They've probably caught him by now.

> **AMIR**
> Who?

> **MERCHANT**
> The big boys chasing him.

EXT. SIDE STREET – DUSK

Amir runs down a rutted road that bounds a neighborhood of flat-ceilinged mud shacks separated by narrow alleys.

The sound of KITE RUNNERS whooping and running fades away in the distance.

Voices filter out from one of these alleys.

> **ASSEF (O.S.)**
> Where's your slingshot now, Hazara? Eh? You don't look so brave today.

Amir creeps down the dark alley, the voices growing louder.

> **ASSEF (O.S.)**
> But I'm in a mood to forgive. What do you say to that, boys?

Ext. Blind Alley – Dusk

A havoc of scrap and rubble litters the alley.

> **KAMAL (O.S.)**
> Very generous. Especially after the rude manners he showed last time.

Amir creeps closer. He holds his breath and peeks around the corner.

Hassan stands at the blind end of the alley in a defiant stance, gripping the blue kite tightly.

Blocking Hassan's way out of the alley are the three bullies encountered earlier: Wali on one side, Kamal on the other, Assef towering in the middle.

Assef seems relaxed, confident.

> **ASSEF**
> Forgiven. It's done.

Amir exhales quietly. He doesn't move from his hiding place.

> **ASSEF**
> Of course, nothing is free in this world. My pardon comes with a small price.

> **WALI**
> Nothing is free.

ASSEF
You're a lucky Hazara. Because today, it's only going to cost you that kite. Fair deal. What do you think, boys?

KAMAL
More than fair.

HASSAN
Amir agha won the tournament and I ran this kite for him. This is his kite.

ASSEF
Loyal Hazara. Loyal dog.

Kamal laughs, shrill and nervous.

ASSEF
Before you sacrifice yourself for him, think about this: Would he do the same for you? Have you ever wondered why he only plays with you when no one else is around?

Assef pauses and studies Hassan's face.

ASSEF
I said, "Why," Hazara!
   (beat)
Because to him, you're nothing but an ugly pet. Something he can play with when he's bored, something he can kick when he's angry.

HASSAN
Amir agha and I are friends.

ASSEF
   (snorting)
Friends? You fool. Enough of this. Give us that kite.

Hassan stoops and picks up a rock. Assef flinches, taking a step backwards.

ASSEF
Last chance.

Hassan cocks the arm holding the rock.

> **ASSEF**
>
> As you wish.

Amir opens his mouth. He's on the verge of calling out, of shouting in protest.

Instead he does nothing. He watches, stiff with fear.

Assef motions with his hand and the other two boys separate, forming a half circle, trapping Hassan in the alley.

> **ASSEF**
>
> Keep it. So it always reminds you of what I'm about to do.

> **WALI**
>
> Nothing is free.

Assef charges. Hassan throws the rock. It strikes Assef on the forehead. Assef yelps as he flings himself at Hassan, knocking him to the ground.

Wali and Kamal follow. The three of them pound Hassan, punching him in the face, kicking him in the ribs. Hassan struggles desperately but he's far too small, far too weak.

Amir retreats behind the wall. He shuts his eyes and bites down on his fist. The sounds of the beating wash over him, the cries of pain, the slap of knuckles on skin.

For a long time Amir doesn't move. Finally the noises quiet. Only muffled voices can be heard from the alley. Amir opens his eyes and peers around the corner again.

ASSEF
He's just a servant's son.

Hassan lies with his chest pinned to the ground, naked from the waist down. Kamal and Wali each grip one of his arms, bent at the elbow so that Hassan's hands are pressed to his back.

WALI
I'm not sure, Assef. My father says it's wrong.

ASSEF
Your father's a Communist.

Assef pulls Hassan's pants down.

ASSEF
And there's nothing wrong about teaching this donkey a lesson.

Assef unbuckles his pants.

ASSEF
Just hold him down.

Assef kneels behind Hassan, puts his hands on Hassan's hips and lifts his bare buttocks.

He positions himself behind Hassan.

Hassan doesn't struggle. Doesn't whimper. His face is blank.

EXT. NARROW STREETS – DUSK

Amir runs—away from the alley, away from Assef's quick, rhythmic grunts, away from Hassan's silence.

Ext. Bazaar - Later

Amir hides in a stairway of the deserted bazaar, crouched beside the padlocked swinging doors.

Hearing voices and running footfalls, he ducks out of sight of Assef and his crew sprinting past, laughing.

KAMAL
Let's get out of here!

Amir takes several deep breaths. He waits until Assef and the others are well out of earshot.

In the dimming light, Hassan trudges toward him.

Hassan holds the blue kite in his hands. His *chapan* has mud smudges down the front. His shirt is ripped below the collar.

He sways on his feet as if he's about to collapse. Finally Amir stands and rushes up to him.

AMIR
Where were you? I was looking for you.

He steadies himself and hands Amir the kite.

Hassan begins to say something but his voice cracks.

HASSAN
Let's go, Agha sahib will worry.

He limps toward home. Amir stares after him. Tiny drops of blood fall from between Hassan's legs, staining the snow.

INT. LIVING ROOM – NIGHT

Amir opens the door and steps inside, carrying the blue kite. Baba drinks tea, reading a book.

Baba smiles, standing, and opens his arms.

BABA
Good job. Come here.

Amir walks into his father's embrace. Baba takes his son's face in his hands with pride.

BABA
Well done.

EXT. BABA'S HOUSE – MORNING

Icicles hang from the eaves, dripping in the sun.

INT. DINING ROOM – MORNING

Amir sits at the table. Hassan is nowhere in sight.

Ali walks in, carrying Amir's breakfast.

AMIR
Where's Hassan?

ALI
He went back to sleep. The last few weeks, all he wants to do is sleep. After chores he just crawls under his blanket.

Ali sets out the food.

ALI

 Can I ask you something?

Amir stares at his plate and says nothing.

ALI

Did something happen, Amir agha? Something he's not telling me?

AMIR

How should I know? Maybe he's sick. People get sick, you know.

INT. STUDY – NIGHT

Baba reads the newspaper, sipping from his whiskey and soda. Amir does his homework. A well-stoked fire burns in the fireplace. Baba groans at something he reads in the paper.

BABA

The mullahs want to rule our souls and the Communists tell us we don't have any.

Baba lowers the paper and studies his son, smiling.

BABA

More importantly, El Cid is playing tomorrow. Tell Hassan to come with us.

Amir turns around.

AMIR

He's not feeling well.

Baba's brow furrows with worry.

BABA

Really? What's wrong with him?

AMIR

He's got a cold or something. Ali says he's sleeping it off.

Baba considers Amir for a moment.

BABA

I haven't seen you two playing together in weeks. What happened?

AMIR

Nothing. He's just been a little sick.

BABA

Hassan never gets sick.
 (beat)
Whatever's going on, you should deal with it before too long. Don't let these things fester. Time will only make it worse.

EXT. CEMETERY – LATER

Amir climbs the hill to the cemetery. He stops beside the low stone wall when he sees Hassan sitting alone in the shade of the pomegranate tree. Dozens of overripe pomegranates have fallen to the ground.

Hassan is trying to read from a children's book. Reading is clearly a struggle for him; he mouths the words, pronouncing them slowly.

Amir steps over the crumbling wall and approaches Hassan, who looks up and smiles when he sees Amir.

AMIR

What are you reading?

HASSAN

(embarrassed)
It's for little kids. I just. . . I'm trying to learn.

Amir nods and says nothing.

HASSAN

I'd rather hear one of your stories.

AMIR

I'm done making up stories.

HASSAN

Why?

AMIR

Because they're stupid.

HASSAN

I don't think they're stupid. I love your stories.

Amir stares at Hassan for a long count. He picks up one of the fallen pomegranates.

AMIR

What would you do if I hit you with this?

Hassan's smile wilts. He looks older, somehow, as if the question had aged him before our eyes.

AMIR

What would you do?

Hassan does not answer, but stands up. Amir hurls the pomegranate. It explodes against Hassan's chest with a spray of red pulp.

AMIR

Hit me back!

Hassan looks at the red stain and then at Amir.

AMIR

Hit me back!

Hassan stands, dazed, unsure what is happening or why. Amir picks up another pomegranate and whips it at Hassan.

AMIR

Hit me back! Hit me back!

Amir picks up another fruit and throws it, and then another, and then another, throwing all the pomegranates he can find, splattering Hassan's body and face with red juice.

AMIR

You're a coward!

When Amir finally stops, exhausted and panting, Hassan, smeared in red, looks like he's been shot by a firing squad.

Hassan stoops to pick up a pomegranate. He walks to Amir, tearing the fruit open in his hands. Hassan crushes the pomegranate against his own forehead. Juice drips down his face. He turns and walks away from Amir, down the hill.

Amir stares after him, tears filling his eyes.

EXT. BABA'S HOUSE – DAY

SALAHUDDIN, a butcher, slaughters a calf in

the shade of a poplar tree, soaking the grass with fresh blood. Two sheep, tied to the tree trunk, grimly await execution.

WORKMEN climb the oak trees, stringing coils of small electric bulbs. Others set up tables in the yard, while CARPENTERS build a stage on a balcony overlooking the garden.

Amir stands beside his father, watching with horror.

BABA
Blood's good for the tree.

Baba sees the queasy look on Amir's face and smiles.

BABA
Come on, birthday boy. Let's go inside.

He puts his hand on Amir's shoulder and leads him toward the house. On their way, Amir sees Hassan and Ali spreading tablecloths on the tables.

BABA
Ali, is everything ready?

ALI
Don't worry, it will be soon.

Hassan looks at Amir and Amir averts his eyes. Baba instructs a WORKER hanging lights.

BABA
Move it back a little.

WORKER
Yes, of course.

Baba and Amir climb the steps toward the front door.

INT. BABA'S HOUSE – CONTINUOUS

Amir closes the door behind them.

> **AMIR**
> Baba, have you ever thought about getting new servants?

Baba pauses on the stairs, startled. He approaches Amir.

> **BABA**
> Why would I want to do that?

> **AMIR**
> *(already regretting it)*
> I guess you wouldn't. It was just a question.

> **BABA**
> I grew up with Ali. My father took him in, loved him like his own son. Forty years he's been with my family. Forty goddamn years. And you think I'm just going to throw him out?

Baba's face is flushed with anger. Amir looks down.

> **BABA**
> I've never laid a hand on you, but you ever say that again. . .
> *(shaking his head)*
> You bring me shame. And Hassan. . . Hassan's not going anywhere. Do you understand?
> *(furious)*
> I said, do you understand?

> **AMIR**
> Yes, Baba.

Baba walks up the stairs, past the framed blue kite, no longer looking at his son.

> **BABA**
> You bring me shame.

INT. BABA'S HOUSE – NIGHT

The place is packed. GUESTS with drinks in hand mingle in the hallways, smoke on the stairs, lean against doorways.

EXT. BABA'S HOUSE – NIGHT

GUESTS chatter under the glow of red, blue, and green lights winking in the trees. Kerosene torches burn on stakes. AHMAD ZAHIR plays a keyboard and sings on the stage as DANCERS spin on a parquet dance floor.

Amir walks through the crowd beside Baba, greeting his guests, a plastered smile on his face. He kisses cheeks, hugs older women, shakes hands. Amir shakes hands, is kissed on the head.

> **ALI**
> Amir agha. . .

Amir turns and sees Ali, Hassan's father, standing nervously on the fringes of the crowd. He looks out of place amongst these well-heeled folks, wearing a threadbare old suit.

Amir nods awkwardly, feeling suddenly guilty in the older man's presence.

Ali hands the boy a box.

> **ALI**
> It is modest and not worthy of you. Happy birthday.

Amir opens the box. Inside is a deluxe edition of the Shahnahmah, with an embossed cover and glossy color illustrations. He stares at the book, unsure how to react.

> **ALI**
> Hassan said your copy was getting old, missing some pages.

Amir cannot meet the older man's eye.

> **AMIR**
> Thank you.

> **ASSEF (O.S.)**
> Happy birthday, Amir jan.

Assef stands with his father, MAHMOOD, a small, dark-skinned man. Amir freezes. Assef notes Amir's fear and grins.

MAHMOOD
Happy Birthday. What a splendid suit.

Baba, concerned that his son seems rude, gives Amir a stern look before smiling at Assef and Mahmood.

ASSEF
Great party, Amir jan.

Amir says nothing, still staring at the ground.

BABA
Aren't you going to thank Assef jan?

AMIR
Thank you.

Amir steps away, unable to stand in the little circle any longer. He squirms through the throng of guests, ignoring the people who pat his back or call out "Happy Birthday."

Baba, annoyed and embarrassed, watches him go.

BABA
(to Mahmood)
Please, enjoy.

Ext. Riverside - Night

Amir sits by the bank of the narrow river behind Baba's house, looking at the ground.

RAHIM KHAN (O.S.)
Shouldn't you be entertaining your guests?

Rahim Khan walks over, ice clinking in his glass.

Production design by Carlos Conti;
graphic illustration by Maud Gircourt.

AMIR

I didn't know you drank.

Rahim Khan sits beside Amir and examines his glass.

RAHIM KHAN

Turns out I do.
(elbowing Amir)
But only on the most important occasions.

Amir smiles. Rahim Khan raises his glass, toasting the birthday boy, and drinks.

RAHIM KHAN

You know, you can tell me anything you want, Amir jan. Anytime.

AMIR

(uncertain)
I know.

Rahim Khan watches Amir, waiting, his black eyes bottomless.

RAHIM KHAN

Here. I almost forgot.

He hands Amir a beautiful leather-bound notebook.

RAHIM KHAN

For your stories.

Before Amir can thank him, explosions rip through the sky. They look up and see fireworks lighting the night. Rahim Khan smiles and helps Amir to his feet.

RAHIM KHAN

Come. You're missing your party.

EXT. BABA'S HOUSE – NIGHT

Amir and Rahim Khan walk through the gates. All the guests dance as the flares sizzle and explode into bouquets of flowers.

Amir sees Hassan serving drinks to Assef and Wali from a silver platter, then walking sullenly away.

INT. AMIR'S ROOM – DAY

A pile of presents occupies one corner of the room: a Polaroid camera; a cricket bat; envelopes stuffed with cash.

Amir sits at the window and inspects a wristwatch with a blue face and gold hands shaped like lightning bolts.

He looks outside.

EXT. BABA'S HOUSE – MORNING

Ali and Hassan walk out the house gates, pushing empty wheelbarrows as they head to market.

INT. STUDY – DAY

Baba sits at his desk, signing various documents as a radio plays news reports in the background.

AMIR (O.S.)
Baba?

Baba looks up and sees his son standing in the doorway.

> **AMIR**
> Have you seen my watch anywhere?

> **BABA**
> The one I just bought you? Don't tell me you already lost it.

> **AMIR**
> No. . . I know I had it in my room.

Baba returns his attention to his papers.

> **BABA**
> I'm sure it'll turn up somewhere.

EXT. BABA'S HOUSE – MOMENTS LATER

Amir crosses the yard and steps inside the servants' hut.

INT. SERVANTS' HUT – CONTINUOUS

Amir lifts Hassan's pillow and plants the watch under it.

INT. BABA'S HOUSE – LATER

Amir knocks on the door of the study.

> **BABA (O.S.)**
> Come in.

INT. STUDY – CONTINUOUS

Amir steps inside. Baba signs papers at his desk. He looks up at Amir's grim face.

> **BABA**
> What's wrong?

Int. Amir's Room – Later

Through his window, Amir watches Ali and Hassan push their wheelbarrows full of meat, naan, and fruit up the driveway.

Baba emerges from the house and walks up to Ali.

BABA

Ali. When you finish your work, come inside with Hassan.

ALI

Yes, Agha Sahib.

INT. LIVING ROOM – DAY

Hassan and Ali stand before Baba. From their red, puffed-up eyes, it seems that Hassan and Ali have both been crying. Amir sits on the leather sofa.

BABA

Did you steal Amir's watch, Hassan?

Hassan looks at Amir, who studies the rug intently. Hassan looks at him for a long time before lowering his eyes.

HASSAN

Yes.

Amir closes his eyes. Ali shakes his head, angry. Baba nods.

BABA

I forgive you.

Amir looks up, stunned to hear his father give pardon.

ALI

We're leaving, Agha sahib.

BABA

What?

ALI

We can't live here anymore.

BABA

But I forgive him, Ali. Didn't you hear?

ALI

Life here is impossible for us now, Agha sahib. We're leaving.

Ali curls his arm around his son's shoulder. He glances at Amir and there is something cold and unforgiving in his eyes.

Baba spreads open his arms, his palms up.

BABA

I don't care about the watch. I don't understand why you're doing this. . .

ALI

I'm sorry, Agha sahib, but our bags are already packed. We've made our decision.

Baba looks lost, a sheen of grief spreading across his face.

BABA

Ali, haven't I provided for you? Haven't I been good to you and Hassan?

Hassan's head is downcast, his shoulders slumped.

BABA

At least tell me why.

Ali shakes his head. His arm around his son's shoulders, he turns and leads Hassan to the door.

BABA

I forbid you to do this! Do you hear me? I forbid you!

Ali stops at the doorway and looks back at Baba.

ALI

Respectfully, you can't forbid me anything, Agha sahib. We don't work for you anymore.

INT. AMIR'S ROOM – DAY

Amir watches through his window as Ali and Hassan walk across the little bridge, carrying their flimsy suitcases.

In the courtyard down below, Baba closes the iron gate and walks back to the house.

Hassan turns and gives the house a final look. Amir edges away from the window, hiding from sight.

EXT. KABUL – NIGHT

A crescent moon shines on the mosques and slender minarets. RUSSIAN SOLDIERS with AK-47s patrol the deserted street. Explosions ignite the darkness.

TITLE CARD: Soviet Invasion, December 1979

INT. AMIR'S ROOM – NIGHT

Amir sleeps through the noise. Baba opens the bedroom door and snaps the light on, awakening him. He sits up and stares out the window, confused and disoriented.

> **BABA**
> Pack a bag. Only what you need. Hurry up!

EXT. JADEH MAYWAND AVENUE – NIGHT

An Armored Personnel Carrier weaves through the outdoor market, past the empty stalls.

INT. LIVING ROOM – NIGHT

Baba sits behind his desk, trying his telephone. Rahim Khan stands at the window, listening to the tanks and soldiers throughout the city.

> **BABA**
> They'll come for me.

> **RAHIM KHAN**
> We don't know that.

> **BABA**
> Read your history, my friend. By the time we know it, it will be too late.
> *(weary smile)*
> You know how I am. You know how I talk. Everyone in Kabul has heard me cursing the Communists.

Baba begins removing the framed photographs from the wall. He stares at the face of his dead wife on their wedding day before glancing up at Rahim Khan.

> **BABA**

Will you watch over the house for me? We'll be back when the Russians leave.

> **RAHIM KHAN**
> What if they don't leave?

> **BABA**
> Everyone leaves. This country is not kind to invaders.

> **RAHIM KHAN**
> And you, my friend? Where will you go?

Int. Amir's Room – Continuous

Amir takes one last look at the pile of toys and the framed photographs of his family.

He leaves all of these behind, taking only two books: the *Shahnamah* and the leather-bound notebook Rahim Khan gave him. He slips them in his suitcase.

> **BABA (O.S.)**
> Pakistan, first. After that. . . wherever is safest for the boy.

INT. LIVING ROOM – CONTINUOUS

Rahim Khan faces Baba.

> **RAHIM KHAN**
> The smugglers want five thousand a head for safe passage to Pakistan. And I'm fairly sure they won't take checks.

Baba scoops a set of keys off the desk.

> **BABA**
> What about a Mustang?

EXT. BABA'S HOUSE – NIGHT

The lights inside shut off.

EXT. RURAL ROAD – DAWN

An old Russian truck motors down the road.

EXT. CHECKPOINT – DAY

The old truck pulls up to a Russian Army check-point.

INT. TRUCK – DAY

Boot heels click on asphalt. KARIM the driver flings open the tarpaulin covering the back of the truck. He and the Russian soldier peer inside.

A dozen PASSENGERS are crammed onto fac-ing benches in the back of the truck, beneath a heavy canvas tarpaulin. They sit with their suit-cases tucked between their legs.

Amir sits beside Baba. Across from them sits a BURLY MAN and his YOUNG WIFE, an INFANT cradled under her arm.

Karim is a scrawny man with a pencil-thin mus-tache. The Russian has the face of a bulldog. A cigarette dangles from his lips.

His eyes settle on the young wife caring for the infant. He speaks in Russian to Karim. Karim answers with a curt reply. The soldier shouts something that makes Karim flinch.

Karim clears his throat and drops his head.

> **KARIM**
> He wants a half hour with the lady in the back of the truck.

The young wife pulls the shawl down over her face. She begins to sob. The husband stares ner-vously at the automatic holstered on the soldier's hip.

> **BURLY MAN**
> What? No. Brother. Please, ask Mister Sol-dier Sahib to show a little mercy.
> *(getting desperate)*
> Maybe he has a wife, too.

Karim cannot look the husband in the eye.

> **KARIM**
> It's his price for letting us pass.

Baba stands. Amir grabs his leg, trying to keep Baba from interfering, but Baba shakes his leg free. He speaks to Karim but looks directly at the Russian.

> **BABA**
> I want you to ask this man something. Ask him where his shame is.

Karim translates and the Russian responds.

> **KARIM**
> He says there is no shame in war.

> **BABA**
> Tell him he's wrong. War doesn't negate decency.

The soldier speaks to Karim, a smile creasing his lips.

> **KARIM**
> Agha sahib, these Roussi are not like us. They understand nothing about respect, honor.

> **BABA**
> What did he say?

> **KARIM**
> He says he'd enjoy putting a bullet in you almost as much as he'd enjoy her.

> **BABA**
> I'll take a thousand of his bullets before I let this indecency take place.

Amir tugs on Baba's sleeve.

> **AMIR**
> Baba, please. He'll shoot you.

Baba pushes Amir back in his seat.

> **BABA**
> Have I taught you anything?
> *(turning to the soldier)*
> Tell him he'd better kill me good with that first shot. Because if I don't go down, I'm tearing him to pieces, goddamn his father!

The soldier flicks away his unfinished cigarette and unholsters his pistol. The Russian raises his automatic.

RUSSIAN OFFICER (O.S.)
Octahobka!

The soldier turns and sees a gray-haired OFFICER hurrying toward them. The soldier rolls his eyes and holsters his gun. The officer glares at the soldier and looks inside the truck, making sure that no one's been shot.

The officer yells at his subordinate in Russian before turning to Karim and waving his hand.

RUSSIAN OFFICER
Go, go.

Karim jogs to the truck's cab, hops in, and shifts into gear. Baba sits, never taking his eyes off the young soldier.

INT. TRUCK – LATER

The passengers ride in silence. Suddenly the burly man stands, walks over to Baba, crouches, and kisses his hand.

BURLY MAN
You are very kind.

BABA
It's not worthy of a thank you.

EXT. JALALABAD – NIGHT

The truck has stopped at the intersection of two dirt roads. Karim throws open the tarpaulin. The passengers step out.

KARIM
Get out. Come on, get out. Keep it moving. Keep it moving.

BABA
Why did you stop?

KARIM
We can't get you across the border in that truck. We don't have enough money to bribe all the Russians.

Baba glares at the smaller man, smelling a swindle.

BABA
So what are we doing?

KARIM
Go climb into that vehicle.

Karim gestures to the end of the street, where an old fuel truck waits.

BABA
You're joking.

KARIM
Your choice, Agha sahib.

EXT. KARIM'S HOUSE – LATER

One by one the refugees mount the idling truck's rear deck, climb the access ladder, and slide down into the empty tank.

KARIM (O.S.)
Climb up quickly.

Baba fishes the snuffbox from his pocket. He empties the box and picks up a handful of Afghani dirt from the unpaved road. He kisses the dirt, pours it into the box, and stows the box in his breast pocket, next to his heart.

Amir climbs the ladder and hesitates by the dark maw of the tank. Inside is pitch black, a steel coffin. Baba has climbed up behind him. He clamps his big hand on his son's shoulder.

BABA
Turn around and go down. I'm with you. Go.

Amir nods, takes a deep breath and slides into the shadows.

Int. Tanker – Night

Absolute darkness. The sound of the truck's wheels crushing gravel filters through the walls of the tanker. A BABY cries. Men and women softly sob and mutter ancient prayers.

For a long time nothing breaks the dark. And then a small miracle, something glowing green. Baba's wristwatch.

BABA
You see it?

AMIR
Yes.

BABA
Don't be afraid. I'm right here with you.

In the weak green light of the watch, Amir huddles against his father's side. The boy is close to panic.

AMIR
I can't breathe, Baba. . .

BABA
Think of something else. Think of a poem.

AMIR
Rumi?

BABA
You've memorized some, haven't you? I want to hear one.

For a moment Amir is quiet, collecting the words. When he begins to recite, his voice is weak, timid, reflecting the terror of his situation.

AMIR
If we come to sleep, we are His drowsy ones.
And if we come to wake, we are in His Hands.

If we come to sleep, we are His
drowsy ones. And if we come to
wake, we are in His Hands.

If we come to weeping, we are
His cloud full of raindrops. And
if we come to laughing, we are
His lightning in that moment.

If we come to anger and battle,
it is the reflection of His
Wrath. And if we come to peace
and pardon, it is the reflection
of His Love. Who are we in
this complicated world?

BABA
Keep going.

AMIR
If we come to weeping, we are His cloud full of raindrops. And if we come to laughing, we are His lightning in that moment.

BABA
Good job.

EXT. BORDER ROAD – CONTINUOUS

The tanker rolls on through the darkness. Amir's voice gains confidence.

AMIR (O.S.)
If we come to anger and battle, it is the reflection of His Wrath. And if we come to peace and pardon, it is the reflection of His Love. Who are we in this complicated world?

EXT. GAS STATION – DAY

An elevated train rumbles past a run down neighborhood.

TITLE CARD:
Fremont, California, 1988

A '68 Mustang, red and freshly waxed, pulls up to one of the pumps. The driver, a WHITE MAN wearing a leather jacket, steps out of the car and walks into the convenience store.

INT. CONVENIENCE STORE – DAY

Baba, wearing the service station uniform, stands behind bulletproof glass. His face looks pale and drawn under the bright fluorescent lights.

He is older now, somewhat diminished, beard graying, hair thinning.

WHITE MAN
Pack of those.

Baba looks out the window to the parked car.

BABA
Is that your car?

WHITE MAN
Yeah.

Baba hands the man his cigarettes, takes his money, and makes change.

BABA
Beautiful car.

Baba speaks English with a thick accent, sometimes struggling with the words.

WHITE MAN
Thanks.

The white man walks out of the store and Baba watches him walk toward the gleaming Mustang.

INT. CONVENIENCE STORE BATHROOM – DAY

Baba straightens his tie. He wears a brown suit that has seen better days. He studies his reflection in the chipped mirror.

EXT. COMMUNITY COLLEGE – DAY

Graduation day. A stage has been set up on the campus green. The SENIORS march one by one in their gowns and mortarboards, accepting their diplomas from a COLLEGE DEAN.

FAMILY MEMBERS sit on folding chairs on the green, snapping photographs, cheering for their loved ones. Baba is in the crowd, sitting very straight in his brown suit.

The DEAN OF STUDENTS, speaking into a microphone at the lectern, reads off the list of graduating seniors, who step forward as their names are called.

DEAN
Richard Hidalgo. Aaron Hill. Denise Hocking. Jennifer Holliday. Damon Hooper. . .

Amir (24) waits for his name to be called, makes

eye contact with Baba, who watches and waits, deeply proud of his son.

Int. Dive Bar - Night

Baba leads Amir (now wearing pleated slacks and a sports jacket) into a rundown bar. WHITE MEN in baseball hats and wifebeaters play pool. Clouds of cigarette smoke hover over the pool tables. The men stare at the Afghans.

Baba and Amir sit at the bar beside an OLD MAN whose leathery face looks sickly in the blue glow of a Michelob sign. Baba lights a cigarette and addresses the BARTENDER in English:

BABA
Hi.

BARTENDER
Hello.

BABA
Tonight I am very happy. Tonight I drink with my son.

Baba turns to the old man.

BABA
How are you my friend? Have a drink with us. What do you like to drink?

The old man nods and smiles. He has no upper teeth.

OLD MAN
Scotch.

BABA
   (to bartender)
Three scotch please.

AMIR
I'll have a beer instead.

BARTENDER
Budweiser?

AMIR
Sure.

Baba offers the old man a cigarette, insisting he take one.

BABA
My son, the college graduate.

Amir's English is nearly perfect, only a trace of accent:

AMIR
It's just a community college.

BABA
It is college. And someday, Doctor Amir!

The drinks are delivered and Baba lights a cigarette.

AMIR
You know I want to write.

BABA
Write?

AMIR
I don't want to be a doctor.

Baba touches glass with Amir and the old man.

BABA
Cheers.

He downs his beer in one gulp. Looks at the bartender.

BABA
One more sir.
   (to old man)
So instead of being a doctor and saving lives, he wants to make up stories.
   (to Amir)
And for money you can work at the gas station with me. We'll put your diploma on the wall.

AMIR
Whatever you think.

Baba sighs, and turns to the pool table just in time to see one of the players make a tricky bank shot.

BABA

Beautiful! Beautiful shot!

(to Amir)

Did you see that shot?

The pool players turn and stare at Baba.

BABA

(to the bartender)

A pitcher of beer for the gentlemen, please!

INT. DIVE BAR – MOMENTS LATER

BABA

Cheers! My son, he graduates college today.

The pool players raise their beers to Amir, uncomfortable with the attention.

POOL PLAYER #1

Way to go, kid.

Everyone drinks. Baba rises to his feet, beer spilling from his glass onto the sawdust floor.

BABA

Fuck the Russia!

The bar patrons laugh, impressed by the crazy Afghan.

BAR PATRONS
FUCK THE RUSSIA!

Everyone drinks. A country song plays on the jukebox and the crowd grows festive.

Amir smiles, shaking his head. Even here, ten thousand miles from home, Baba is the most popular man in the joint.

Baba drinks his beer and puts his hand on Amir's shoulder.

BABA
I wish Hassan had been with us today. This would make him happy.

The smile fades from Amir's face.

Ext. San Jose Flea Market - Day

Baba and Amir have their own stall in the Used Goods section of the flea market. All the other stalls in their aisle are occupied by Afghans.

Amir runs the stand, collecting ten dollars for the Chicago albums. After giving the buyer his change, Amir sees Baba approaching with an older, distinguished-looking man.

BABA
Amir jan, this is General Sahib, Mr. Iqbal Taheri. He was a decorated general in Kabul.

The general laughs politely. His silver hair is combed back from his smooth, tanned forehead.

He wears a gray three-piece suit, shiny from too many pressings.

GENERAL TAHERI
Such a lofty introduction. *Salaam*, my child.

Amir shakes the general's hand.

AMIR
Salaam, General Sahib.

BABA
Amir is going to be a great writer.

GENERAL TAHERI
Mashallah. Will you be writing about our country? History, perhaps?

AMIR
I write fiction.

GENERAL TAHERI
Ah, a storyteller. Well, people need stories to divert them occasionally.

SORAYA (O.S.)
Padar jan, you forgot your tea.

The men turn. Soraya is a slim-hipped beauty with velvety black hair. She carries an open thermos and a Styrofoam cup.

Amir blinks, staring at her. Her walnut brown eyes, shaded by fanned lashes, meet Amir's, hold for a moment, and look away.

GENERAL TAHERI
You are too kind, my dear.

Soraya turns and heads back to her own family's stall, two aisles away. Amir watches her go.

GENERAL TAHERI
My daughter, Soraya jan.
(beat)
Well, time to go set up.

He shakes Amir's hand.

GENERAL TAHERI
Best of luck with the writing.

Baba shakes The General's hand.

BABA
Until later.

GENERAL TAHERI
Goodbye.

The general leaves them. Baba stares at Amir, smiling.

AMIR
What?

BABA
She has made an impression on you?

AMIR
Please, Baba.

Baba laughs and pours himself another cup of tea.

INT. KITCHEN – NIGHT

Amir types feverishly on an old manual typewriter.

BABA (O.S.)
What are you writing?

Amir looks up and sees Baba standing in the doorway.

AMIR
A story.

Amir smiles and looks at the typed words on the white page.

BABA
Write well.

Baba exits the room, closing the door behind him, leaving his son alone with his typewriter.

EXT. BABA AND AMIR'S STALL – DAY

Amir counts their earnings: fives, singles, and coins.

BABA
How much?

AMIR
One hundred and sixty.

BABA
Not bad.

Amir stands and stretches.

AMIR
Do you want a Coke?

BABA
Sure. Be careful.

AMIR
Of what?

BABA
The general is a Pashtun to the root. He has honor and pride.

AMIR
I was only going to get us Cokes.

BABA
Just don't embarrass me, that's all I ask.

AMIR
I won't.

Ext. Soraya's Booth - Moments Later

Soraya reads a book behind a table covered with old curling irons and neckties. She looks up when Amir approaches.

AMIR
Hi.

SORAYA
Hi.

She waits for more and Amir struggles to think of something.

AMIR
Is General Sahib here today?

SORAYA
Yeah. He went that way.

Soraya points.

AMIR
Will you tell him I stopped by to pay my respects?

SORAYA
I will.

AMIR
Thank you.

Amir nods and smiles and Soraya stares at him, not sure if their conversation is over.

AMIR
Oh, and my name is Amir. In case you need to know. So you can tell him. That I stopped by. To. . . pay my respects.

Amir shifts on his feet, clearing his throat. She smiles.

AMIR
I'll go now. Sorry to disturb you.

SORAYA
Oh no, no, no, you didn't.

AMIR
Oh. Good.

Amir begins to walk away but stops and turns around.

AMIR
Can I ask what you're reading?

The words seem to hush the chatter of the nearby Afghans. Their collective focus shifts to Amir and Soraya. Heads turn. Soraya shows the book's cover to Amir. Wuthering Heights.

SORAYA
Have you read it?

AMIR
(nodding)
It's a sad story.

SORAYA
I heard you write.

Amir perks up. He hesitates and goes for broke:

AMIR
Would you like to read one of my stories?

Soraya's eyes flick from side to side nervously.

SORAYA
I'd like that.

Amir nods and smiles. He walks away from her table again, realizes he's heading in the wrong direction, spins around and goes the other way, nodding one last time at Soraya.

INT. KITCHEN – NIGHT

Amir hammers at the keys of his typewriter.

INT. LIVING ROOM – CONTINUOUS

Baba reads a Farsi newspaper and sips from a cup of black tea. He flips the page.

He listens to his son's typing and smiles.

EXT. APARTMENT BUILDING – DAY

Baba carries boxes from their apartment down to their van, parked on the street. While Amir loads the back of the van, Baba has to stop at the bottom of the stairs, struggling for breath.

EXT. SAN JOSE FLEA MARKET – DAY

Amir strides through the aisles, attempting an air of confidence. He holds a roll of stapled pages in one hand.

EXT. SORAYA'S BOOTH – DAY

A POTBELLIED MAN examines a set of pewter candlesticks.

> **POTBELLIED MAN**
> How much?

> **SORAYA**
> Five dollars.

> **POTBELLIED MAN**
> I'll give you three.

> **SORAYA**
> Okay.

The potbellied man fishes out three singles and walks off with his candlesticks. Amir has watched the transaction.

> **AMIR**
> You're not much of a haggler.

Soraya looks up and smiles when she sees Amir.

> **SORAYA**
> I know.

> **AMIR**
> I brought you something.

He hands her the roll of stapled pages.

> **SORAYA**
> You remembered.

> **AMIR**
> Of course.

She looks pleased, holding the story carefully, as if it could shatter if she squeezed too hard. Suddenly her smile vanishes. Her eyes fix on something behind Amir. He turns around, coming face to face with her father.

> **GENERAL TAHERI**
> *(smiling thinly)*
> Amir jan. Our aspiring storyteller. What a pleasure.

> **AMIR**
> *Salaam*, General Sahib.

The general moves past Amir, toward the booth.

> **GENERAL TAHERI**
> What a beautiful day it is, no?

He extends his hand toward Soraya. She gives him the story.

> **GENERAL TAHERI**
> They say it will rain this week. Hard to believe, isn't it?

He drops the rolled pages in the garbage can. Turning back to Amir, he puts a hand on the young man's shoulder and guides him, gently but firmly, away from the stall.

> **GENERAL TAHERI**
> You know, child, I've grown rather fond of you. You're a decent boy, but sometimes, even decent boys need reminding. So it's my duty to remind you that you are among peers.

They stop walking. The general's expressionless eyes bore into Amir's.

> **GENERAL TAHERI**
> Here, everyone here is a storyteller.

The general smiles, revealing perfectly even teeth.

> **GENERAL TAHERI**
> Do pass my respects to your father, Amir jan.

> **AMIR**
> Yes, of course.

EXT. BABA AND AMIR'S STALL – LATER

Baba sells a vintage teddy bear to an ELDERLY WOMAN.

BABA
You have granddaughter? Impossible.

ELDERLY WOMAN
Thank you very much.

The elderly woman laughs and walks away with the teddy bear. Amir returns to the stall, slouched and disconsolate.

BABA
Amir, what's wrong?

AMIR
Nothing.

BABA
The general?
  (*off Amir's nod*)
Akh, Amir.

Baba's about to say something more but he begins to cough. At first Amir, caught up in his own worries, doesn't notice. But when the coughing doesn't stop Amir turns to his father.

AMIR
Baba? Are you alright?

Baba holds up a hand, as if to say, *it's okay*. But the coughing doesn't stop. Amir hurries over to his side. Baba takes deep breaths, holding his son's hand.

Int. Examining Room – Day

Baba sits on the examining table. DR. STARO-BIN listens to his chest with a stethoscope. Baba stares at the doctor. Amir stands to the side, watching.

DR. STAROBIN
Have you been coughing?

BABA
Yes. Where are you from, Doctor?

DR. STAROBIN
Grew up in Michigan. Came out here for medical school. Once you get used to that California sunshine. . .

BABA
But your family?

DR. STAROBIN
Oh, my family. We're originally from Russia.

Baba pushes Dr. Starobin away. He slides off the examining table and grabs his shirt. The doctor, puzzled, stares at Baba and then Amir, who shakes his head in apology.

AMIR
I'm sorry.

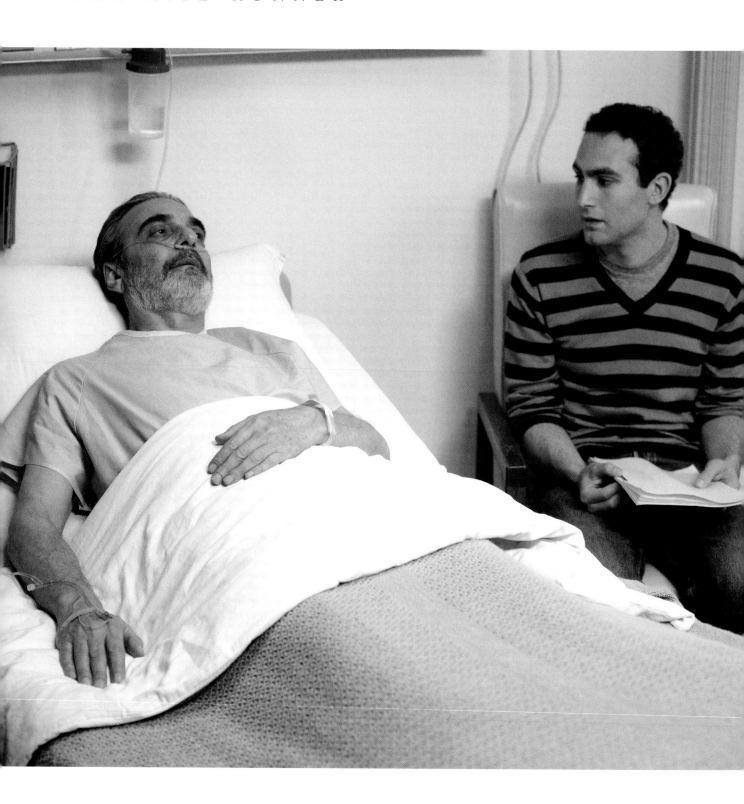

INT. SECOND EXAMINING ROOM – DAY

Baba sits on another examining table while DR. AMANI, an Iranian man with a crooked mustache, listens to Baba's chest with his stethoscope.

Baba smiles beatifically at Amir. Amir rolls his eyes.

INT. DR. AMANI'S OFFICE – DAY

Dr. Amani sits behind his desk, CAT scans and bronchoscopy reports piled before him. Baba and Amir sit across from him.

> **DR. AMANI**
> How are you feeling?
> *(beat)*
> Listen. . . We have your results back.

Baba studies the doctor for a moment. He understands what he is about to hear.

> **BABA**
> *(to Amir)*
> Wait outside for me.

INT. DOCTOR'S WAITING ROOM – DAY

Amir waits nervously for his father. When he sees Baba he stands. Baba motions for them to leave.

> **AMIR (O.S.)**
> "The citizens of Kabul were skeletons now, skeletons selling naswar in the night market, skeletons drinking cups of strong tea, skeletons playing cards in the moonlight."

INT. HOSPITAL ROOM – DAY

Baba lies in bed, an IV line keeping him hydrated. Amir sits in the chair beside him, reading his story.

> **AMIR**
> They greeted me as I passed, teeth clacking together in their jaws. '*Salaam*, brother,' they said. 'Welcome home.'"

Amir looks up from his typed pages, waiting for a response.

> **AMIR**
> It's sort of a work in progress. It's called *The Sultans of Kabul*.

> **BABA**
> Good title. Keep going.

> **AMIR**
> That's the end.

> **BABA**
> That's not an ending.

Amir smiles as he puts the story back in a folder.

> **AMIR**
> It's my story. I get to end it how I want.

A machine beeps. Baba lifts his arm and stares glumly at the plastic tube protruding from his arm.

> **BABA**
> I'm tired of these machines. Tomorrow I want you to take me home.

> **AMIR**
> But Dr. Amani said—

> **BABA**
> *(sharp)*
> It is not Dr. Amani's decision.

A knock on the door. Amir stands as General Taheri, his wife JAMILA, and Soraya enter the room and greet them both.

General Taheri takes Baba's hand.

> **GENERAL TAHERI**
> How are you, my friend?

Baba motions to beeping machine. He smiles thinly. The general smiles back.

> **BABA**
> You shouldn't have burdened yourselves.

JAMILA
It's no burden.

GENERAL TAHERI
No burden at all. If you need anything, ask me like you'd ask a brother.

Baba shakes his head on the pillow.

BABA
Your coming here has brightened my eyes.

The general smiles and squeezes Baba's hand.

GENERAL TAHERI
What about you, Amir jan? Do you need anything?

AMIR
No, thank you, General Sahib.

Amir's voice catches, tears coming to his eyes.

AMIR
Excuse me.

He bolts from the room. Baba keeps his spirits up.

BABA
Thank you. Those are beautiful flowers.

INT. HOSPITAL HALLWAY – MOMENTS LATER

Amir stands by a window. He leans against the railing, trying to control himself, to keep from breaking down. The door to Baba's room opens and Soraya walks out.

SORAYA
I'm really sorry.

Amir tries to smile.

AMIR
You'd better go back inside or your father will come after me.

SORAYA
Your story made me cry.

AMIR
You read it?

SORAYA
Our secret?

AMIR
Yeah. Our secret.

She walks away, leaving Amir smiling improbably in the oncology ward.

INT. BABA'S APARTMENT, LIVING ROOM – NIGHT

Baba lies reading on the couch, a wool blanket covering him. Amir brings him hot tea and a plate of roasted almonds.

Amir sets the dishes on the coffee table. Baba has lost a good deal of weight.

AMIR
Can I do anything else for you?

BABA
No, child. Thank you.

AMIR

Then I wonder if you'll do something for me.

Baba looks up at his son.

AMIR

I want you to go khastegari. I want you to ask General Taheri for his daughter's hand.

Baba's dry lips stretch into a smile.

BABA

Are you sure?

AMIR

More sure than I've ever been about anything.

BABA

Then give me the phone. And my address book.

Amir blinks—he didn't expect it to happen so fast.

AMIR

Now?

BABA

Then when?

Amir smiles.

INT. BABA'S APARTMENT, LIVING ROOM – MOMENTS LATER

Baba is on the phone.

BABA

General Sahib, *Salaam alaykum*. . . yes, much, much better. . . It was gracious of you to come. . . General Sahib, I called to ask. . . if you have the time. . . if I may pay you a visit tomorrow morning. It's an honorable matter. . .

Amir smiles at the turn of events.

INT. BABA'S BEDROOM – MORNING

Sunlight streams in through the windows. Amir helps Baba straighten his worn suit. There is a two-inch gap between the collar button and Baba's neck.

BABA (O.S.)

Nine o'clock? That's just fine. Until then.

EXT. TAHERI'S HOUSE – MORNING

The old beat up van pulls up to the curb. Amir hops down from the driver's seat, walks around to the passenger side and helps Baba out. Once Baba is on his feet he shoos his son away.

BABA

Go home. I'll call you in an hour.

AMIR

Okay. Good luck.

Baba smiles. He turns and hobbles toward the house.

INT./EXT. BABA'S APARTMENT – DAY

Amir, holding a cordless phone, paces back and forth along the walkway on the second floor of his building.

The phone rings. He grabs it immediately.

AMIR
Hello?

BABA (V.O.)
The general accepted.

Amir lets out a burst of air.

AMIR
He accepted?

BABA (V.O.)
Yes, he accepted. But Soraya jan wants to talk to you first.

AMIR
About what?

BABA (V.O.)
About what? How do I know about what? She wants to talk to you.

AMIR
Okay, okay. I'm on my way.

INT. TAHERI'S HOUSE – DAY

Soraya's mother Jamila opens the front door and lets Amir inside. She beams at him.

JAMILA
How are you? Come inside and have some tea.

General Taheri smiles at Amir and shakes his hand.

GENERAL TAHERI
He didn't come for tea.

JAMILA
It doesn't matter, we're going out for a walk.

Ext. Suburban Street – Day

Amir and Soraya walk past small houses with tidy lawns. Neither of them speaks; both look deeply uncomfortable. Amir turns and looks at Jamila, who follows ten paces behind.

AMIR
You do want to get married. To me, I mean?

SORAYA
Of course I do! It's just. . . I want to tell you something. Something you need to know. I don't want us to start with secrets.
    (beat)
We lived in Virginia before we came here. We left because. . . I ran away with an Afghan man. I was eighteen. I guess I thought I was being rebellious. We lived together for almost a month. All the Afghans in Virginia were talking about it.

Soraya peeks at Amir's face, terrified that this news might dissuade him from his proposal.

SORAYA
My father eventually found us. He showed up at the door and. . . made me come home. I was hysterical. And I told him that I hated him.
    (beat)
We moved out to California a few weeks later. I didn't talk to my father for a very long time. And now. . . now I feel like he's the reason why I'm here.

They stop walking. Jamila stops twenty feet behind and pretends to study her neighbor's flower garden.

SORAYA
Does what I told you bother you?

AMIR
A little.

SORAYA
Does it bother you enough to change your mind?

AMIR
No. Not even close. I'd marry you tonight if I could.

Soraya smiles up at him.

INT. BANQUET HALL – NIGHT

Amir, wearing a tuxedo, walks hand in hand with Soraya, who shimmers in a white dress, veiled and lovely. Her hands are painted with henna.

Baba limps along next to Amir; the general and his wife walk beside their daughter.

A procession of UNCLES, AUNTS, and COUS-INS follows the bride and groom as they make their way through the hall, parting a sea of APPLAUDING GUESTS, blinking at flashing cameras.

A YOUNG MAN holds a Koran over the bride and groom's heads as they inch forward. Afghan wedding songs blare from the speakers.

Amir and Soraya slowly make their way to a stage upon which a spotlit sofa sits like a throne.

They sit on the sofa as three hundred faces look on. A cousin hands Amir a mirror. A translucent muslin cloth is thrown over Amir and Soraya's heads.

Under the cloth, the lighting is soft and multi-colored. Amir is careful not to look directly at Soraya yet. Instead he watches in the mirror.

Amir smiles at the beautiful face in the mirror.

SORAYA
What do you see?

AMIR
The rest of my life.

He gently kisses her cheek. The guests applaud.

INT. BANQUET HALL – LATER

The party is in full swing. Guests pick from platters of *chopan* kabob, *sholeh-goshti*, and wild-orange rice.

Sweat-drenched men dance the traditional *attan*

107

What do you see?
The rest of my life.

in a circle, bouncing, spinning faster and faster with the feverish tempo of the tabla.

Amir and Soraya dance and celebrate while Baba sits on the sofa on the stage, smiling at his son, frail but happy.

INT. BABA'S LIVING ROOM – NIGHT

Amir and Soraya sit by the coffee table, flipping through photos from the wedding.

> **SORAYA**
> They're so funny.

> **AMIR**
> They were crazy. There's a funny picture. . .

Baba lies on the couch, under a wool blanket. He watches his son sitting with Soraya.

> **BABA**
> Amir jan. Help me to bed.

> **AMIR**
> Of course.

Soraya and Amir place Baba's frail arms around their shoulders and guide him into the bedroom.

INT. BABA'S BEDROOM – MOMENTS LATER

Soraya and Amir ease Baba into his bed. Soraya switches off the bedside lamp.

> **SORAYA**
> I'll come back with your morphine and a glass of water, Kaka jan.

> **BABA**
> No. There is no pain tonight.

> **BABA**
> *(to Soraya)*
> Come here, my daughter.

Soraya leans close and Baba kisses her forehead. He beckons for Amir and kisses his son's cheek and hugs him.

Amir and Soraya walk out of the room, hand in hand.

Baba watches them go, a small smile on his face.

He reaches for the tin snuffbox he filled with Afghan dirt long ago. He kisses the snuffbox and rests it on his chest as Amir turns out the light and shuts the door.

Ext. Muslim Section, Cemetery - Day

The GRAVEDIGGERS lower a simple wooden casket into the ground. Scores of MOURNERS stand by the open grave, the men on one side (Amir, the general, etc.), the women on the other (Soraya, Jamila, etc.).

A MULLAH recites a Koranic verse. Amir watches the first shovelful of dirt hit the coffin.

CROSSFADE TO:

Amir looks out his apartment window, on the phone.

> **RAHIM KHAN (V.O.)**
> It will not be easy.

INT. AMIR'S APARTMENT – DAY

TITLE CARD:
San Francisco, 2000

His book *A Season for Ashes* rests on the table.

> **RAHIM KHAN (O.S.)**
> But you must come Amir.

AMIR
Alright.

RAHIM KHAN
You're a good man.

AMIR
God willing.

RAHIM KHAN
Goodbye.

AMIR
Goodbye.

Amir lowers the phone into the cradle.

INT. BEDROOM – DAY

Soraya is wearing a bathrobe. Amir walks in and leans against the door frame, a somber expression on his face.

SORAYA
Are you all right?

AMIR
I have to go to Pakistan.

SORAYA
Pakistan?

AMIR
Rahim Khan is very sick.

SORAYA
Your father's friend?
(off Amir's nod)
Is it safe right now?
(beat)
What about your book tour?

AMIR
There wouldn't be any books if not for Rahim Khan.

EXT. STREETS OF PESHAWAR – DAY

TITLE CARD:
Peshawar, Pakistan

A taxicab weaves through a maze of narrow alleys, dodging PEDESTRIANS, BICYCLISTS, and rickshaws popping blue smoke. The cab passes BEARDED VENDORS selling carpets and lampshades, KIDS selling cigarettes, and tiny restaurants with maps of Afghanistan painted on their windows.

INT. TAXICAB – DAY

Amir sits in the backseat of the smoke-filled car, on shredded upholstery. The DRIVER steers with one thumb.

DRIVER
Terrible what's happening in your country. Afghani people and Pakistani people, they're like brothers. Muslims have to help Muslims.

Amir nods politely, staring out the window.

DRIVER
They call this area "Afghan Town." Sometimes it feels like Peshawar is a suburb of Kabul.

He laughs at his own joke and Amir continues to nod politely.

EXT. RAHIM KHAN'S BUILDING – DAY

The cab pulls up to a narrow building on a busy street. Amir steps out of the cab, takes his lone suitcase, and walks up to the hand-carved door.

INT. CORRIDOR – DAY

Amir walks up a dimly lit stairway and knocks.

After a moment, the door swings open. Sickness has dwindled Rahim Khan to skin and bones, but his eyes, sharp and intelligent, are the same. He smiles and embraces Amir.

RAHIM KHAN
Amir jan. Amir jan. Welcome, welcome. You've become a man.

Int. Rahim Khan's apartment - Later

Rahim Khan sits on a wispy mattress set along the wall, looking at a photograph of Soraya. Amir pours two cups of tea from a samovar and brings them over.

RAHIM KHAN
General Taheri's daughter, eh?
  (*handing back the photo*)
She's a beauty. Any children?

AMIR
No.
  (*hesitates*)
We tried, but. . . It doesn't seem possible for us.

Rahim Khan nods, drinking his tea, too courteous to press the matter.

RAHIM KHAN
Thank you.

AMIR
How long have you been in Pakistan?

RAHIM KHAN
Less than a year. Kabul's no longer safe for me.

AMIR
The Taliban are as bad as they say?

RAHIM KHAN
Oh, worse. Much worse. They don't let you be human. They even banned kite flying.

AMIR
  (*remembering*)
I have something for you.

He opens his satchel, pulls out a copy of *A Season for Ashes*, and hands it to Rahim Khan.

RAHIM KHAN
  (*starting to smile*)
What is this?

AMIR
Look. . .

He opens the cover and shows Rahim Khan the dedication page.

RAHIM KHAN
  (*reading in halting English*)
"For Rahim Khan, who listened to my stories before I knew how to write them."

Tears fill Rahim Khan's eyes as he looks at the words.

RAHIM KHAN
  (*looking up at Amir*)
This is a great honor, Amir. Thank you.

AMIR
Let me take you home with me. I can find you a good doctor. They're coming up with new treatments all the time—

RAHIM KHAN
I see America has infused you with her optimism. But there is such a thing as God's will.

Rahim Khan motions for Amir to come closer.

RAHIM KHAN
Come sit. I didn't bring you here to complain about my health. Forgive me Amir jan. . . forgive me for what I have to tell you.
  (*long beat*)
Hassan is dead.

Amir looks away, distraught. He hasn't seen Hassan in twenty-one years but the news devastates him.

AMIR
How?

RAHIM KHAN
You know I watched over your father's house after you left. But none of the caretakers I hired lasted more than a year. Some were dishonest; some lazy. So a few years ago I went to Hazarajat and brought

Hassan and his family home with me. His wife, Farzana. And their son, Sohrab.

AMIR
Rostam and Sohrab.

Rahim stands up and moves to his table.

RAHIM KHAN
It was good to have them there. Hassan kept the house from falling apart; Farzana cooked the meals; it was good. But when my health began to fail. . . well, there isn't a hospital in Afghanistan that can help me. So I came here.

Rahim Khan shrugs and offers a thin smile.

RAHIM KHAN
A few weeks after I left, the Taliban came. Hassan told them that he was looking after the house for me. They said that he was a liar and a thief like all the other Hazaras. And they ordered him to get his family out by nightfall.
  (beat)
Hassan wouldn't leave.

Amir joins Rahim Khan at the table.

RAHIM KHAN
So they took him to the street, and ordered him to kneel. . . And shot him in the back of the head.

Amir averts his eyes, pained by the thought.

RAHIM KHAN
Farzana came screaming and attacked them.
So they shot her, too.

Amir can do nothing but stare at the floor.

AMIR
And the boy? Sohrab?

RAHIM KHAN
He's in an orphanage in Karteh-Seh.

Rahim Khan picks up an envelope from a side table and offers it to Amir.

RAHIM KHAN
Hassan sent this to me a week before he died. It's for you.

Amir looks at his own name, printed in neat Farsi letters on the front of the envelope.

RAHIM KHAN
He taught himself how to read and write.
He didn't want to send you a letter until he could do it properly.

Amir moves to the window, staring at the envelope.

RAHIM KHAN
Amir, you need to go back to Kabul.

Amir, still stunned by the news of his old play-mate's death, doesn't know how to respond.

RAHIM KHAN
I've already arranged for a driver. He's a good man.

AMIR
I. . . I can't go to Kabul. Can't you pay someone here to go? I'll pay for it if it's a matter of money.

RAHIM KHAN
It isn't about money! You are a storyteller.
Some part of you has always known this story. Ali's first wife was from Jagheri.

AMIR
What does that have to do with anything?

RAHIM KHAN
After five years she left him childless and married a man in Khost. She bore that man three daughters. Do you understand what I'm trying to tell you? Ali was sterile.

AMIR
But he had Hassan.

RAHIM KHAN
He raised Hassan. He didn't father him.
     (*beat*)
Your father loved you both. Because you were both his sons. And Sohrab—

AMIR
No.

RAHIM KHAN
He's your nephew.

AMIR
I don't believe you.

RAHIM KHAN
You *do*. That's what frightens you.

AMIR
You're saying my father. . . for all those years. . . lied to me.

RAHIM KHAN
Please think, Amir jan. All that a man had back then was his honor, his name, and if people talked—

AMIR
He lied to me.

RAHIM KHAN
He lied to both of you. And now there's a way to be good again.

EXT. STREETS OF PESHAWAR – DAY

Amir walks down a noisy lane choked with

PEDESTRIANS and rickshaws, the walls plastered with Lollywood movie posters.

Int. Tea House - Day

Amir sits at a table by himself, looking at the unopened envelope in his hands. Finally he tears it open and pulls out a Polaroid and a folded letter.

INSERT POLAROID

A tall man in a green-striped chapan stands with a little boy in front of the wrought-iron gates of Baba's house. Twenty years later Hassan still has the same narrow green eyes.

The boy, Sohrab, looks exactly the same as Hassan did at that age, shaved head and all.

END INSERT

Amir begins reading the neatly-composed Dari letter.

> **AMIR (V.O.)**
> *In the name of Allah the most beneficent, the most merciful, Amir agha, with my deepest respects. My wife and son and I pray this letter finds you in fine health and in the light of*

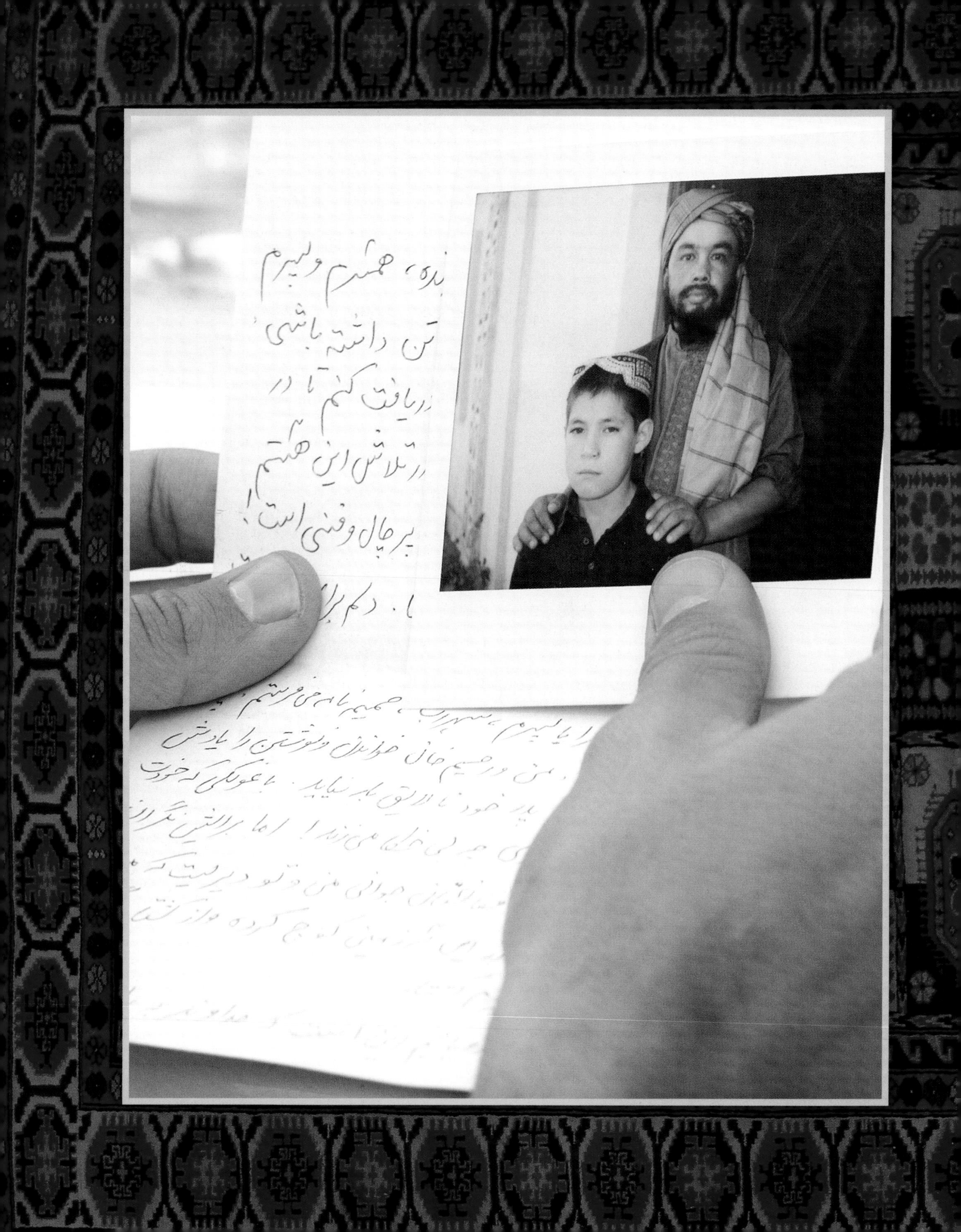

In the name of Allah the most beneficent, the most merciful. Amir agha, with my deepest respects. My wife and son and I pray this letter finds you in fine health and in the light of Allah's good graces. I am hopeful that one day I will hold one of your letters in my hands and read of your life in America. I am trying to learn English. It is such a tricky language! But one day, agha. I miss your stories.

I have included a picture of me and my son, Sohrab. He is a good boy. Rahim Khan and I taught him how to read and write so he does not grow up stupid like his father. And can he shoot with that slingshot you gave me! But I fear for him, Amir agha.

The Afghanistan of our youth is long dead. Kindness is gone from the land and you cannot escape the killings. Always the killings.

I dream that Allah will guide us to a better day. I dream that my son will grow up to be a good person, a free person, an important person. I dream that flowers will bloom in the streets of Kabul again and music will play in the samovar houses and kites will fly in the skies. And I dream that someday you will return to Kabul to revisit the land of our childhood.

If you do, you will find an old faithful friend waiting for you. May Allah be with you always.   Hassan.

Allah's good graces. I am hopeful that one day I will hold one of your letters in my hands and read of your life in America. I am trying to learn English. It is such a tricky language! But one day, agha. I miss your stories.

Amir shakes his head, his eyes gone glassy with tears.

AMIR (V.O.)

I have included a picture of me and my son, Sohrab. He is a good boy. Rahim Khan and I taught him how to read and write so he does not grow up stupid like his father. And can he shoot with that slingshot you gave me! But I fear for him, Amir agha.

A rickshaw turns sharply and spills bushels of apples on the street.

AMIR (V.O.)

The Afghanistan of our youth is long dead. Kindness is gone from the land and you cannot escape the killings. Always the killings.

Flashes of young Hassan with his kite imprint his mind. Amir covers his eyes with one hand, unable to continue for a moment. Merchants pick up the spilled apples.

After taking a deep breath he finishes the letter.

AMIR (V.O.)

I dream that Allah will guide us to a better day. I dream that my son will grow up to be a good person, a free person, an important person. I dream that flowers will bloom in the streets of Kabul again and music will play in the samovar houses and kites will fly in the skies. And I dream that someday you will return to Kabul to revisit the land of our childhood.

More visions of young Hassan and his kite. Happy in the past.

ADULT HASSAN

If you do, you will find an old faithful friend

waiting for you. May Allah be with you always. Hassan.

Amir studies the photograph again.

Ext. Cafe – Day

Amir stands outside, using the cafe's phone.

INT. AMIR'S APARTMENT – NIGHT

Soraya picks up the ringing phone.

SORAYA

Hello?

EXT. CAFE – CONTINUOUS

AMIR

Hi. Did I wake you up?

INT. AMIR'S APARTMENT – CONTINUOUS

SORAYA

No. Are you alright?

EXT. CAFE – CONTINUOUS

AMIR

(*long beat*)
I have to tell you a story.

INT. AMIR'S APARTMENT – NIGHT

The lights of San Francisco glitter outside the window. Soraya sits in a chair, the phone held to her ear. As the camera pushes in, we see that she has been listening for a long time. Tears streak her cheeks.

SORAYA

What's his name?

EXT. KHYBER PASS – DAY

An old Land Cruiser, body pockmarked with dime-sized rust holes, motors past a bullet-riddled sign that reads: *The Khyber Pass Welcomes You.*

The road ahead winds through cliffs of shale and limestone.

Int. Land Cruiser – Day

Amir sits in the passenger seat wearing the garb of a native Afghan (the kind of garb he never wore when he actually lived in Afghanistan): a rough wool blanket wrapped over a gray *pirhan-tumban* and a vest.

He also wears an expertly-crafted fake beard—if we didn't know him we could never spot it for a fake.

The driver, FARID, is a lanky, bearded Tajik with narrow shoulders and a weather-beaten face. He clutches a cigarette between the two remaining fingers of his maimed left hand.

Amir scratches at the underside of his fake beard, where it itches.

Farid has barely glanced at Amir this whole time. He doesn't look at him now as he gives an order.

> **FARID**
> Stop playing with it.

> **AMIR**
> I really have to wear it?

Now Farid turns and glares at Amir.

> **FARID**
> You know what the Taliban will do to you if they see you're clean-shaven?

Amir stops touching the scratchy beard.

EXT. BORDER CROSSING – LATER

The Land Cruiser slows to a stop. A guard hut flanks the road. A PAKISTANI SOLDIER approaches. Farid offers papers but the soldier, after a cursory glance inside, waves them on.

Farid

EXT. DESERT – CONTINUOUS

The Land Cruiser passes the ruined remnants of a village. Smoke still rises from the rubble.

Amir stares at the tuft of blackened, roofless walls.

EXT. SAND DUNES – DAY

The Land Cruiser rolls past an endless expanse of dunes.

INT. LAND CRUISER – DAY

> **FARID**
> So what brings you back to Afghanistan? Come to sell off your father's land? Pocket the money?
>
> **AMIR**
> I'm not here to sell anything. I'm going to Kabul to find a boy.
>
> **FARID**
> A boy?

Amir fishes the Polaroid from the pocket of his shirt. He hands it to Farid, who holds it over the steering wheel and examines it. He looks from Amir to the photo and back again.

> **FARID**
> This boy?

(off Amir's nod)
This Hazara boy?

> **AMIR**
> Yeah.
>
> **FARID**
> What's he mean to you?
>
> **AMIR**
> His father meant a lot to me. He's the man in the photo. He's dead now.
>
> **FARID**
> He was a friend of yours?

For a moment Amir is silent, staring out the window.

> **AMIR**
> He was my brother.

Farid sighs, watching the road unroll before them.

EXT. DESTROYED ROAD – DAY

The Land Cruiser lurches over the ravaged old highway leading to Kabul. Land mines and artillery shells have left massive craters that Farid needs to steer around.

> **AMIR**
> I feel like a tourist in my own country.

Do you remember what
this street smelled
like in the old days?
Lamb kabobs.

FARID
You've always been a tourist here. You just didn't know it.

AMIR
What happened to the trees?

FARID
The Russians chopped them down.

CHILDREN dressed in rags chase a soccer ball. A cluster of MEN sit on the carcass of a burned-out Soviet tank.

EXT. KITE SQUARE – DAY

The Land Cruiser drives west. To the north is the bone-dry Kabul River. On the hills to the south stands the broken old city wall. A haze of dust hovers over the city.

Entire blocks have been obliterated to rubble. The buildings that haven't entirely collapsed are barely standing, with caved-in roofs and walls pierced with rocket shells.

A bullet-pocked sign is half-buried in a heap of debris: Drink Coca Co-

CHILDREN play in the ruins of a windowless building amid jagged stumps of brick and stone. BICYCLISTS and mule-drawn carts swerve around kids, stray dogs, and piles of debris.

BEGGARS squat on every corner, dressed in shredded burlap rags, mud-caked hands held out for a coin. Many of them are very young, sitting in the laps of their burqa-clad MOTHERS.

INT. LAND CRUISER – CONTINUOUS

A block north, two MEN argue on a street corner. One of them hobbles on his lone good leg. The other leg is amputated below the knee. He cradles an artificial leg in his arms.

FARID
You know what they're doing?

AMIR
He's selling his leg?

FARID
You can get good money for it. Feed your kids for a couple of weeks.

EXT. KITE SQUARE – DAY

Amir and Farid step out of the parked Land Cruiser, not far from the location of Saifo's kite store.

AMIR
What's that smell?

FARID
Diesel. The power's always going off so people use generators.

AMIR
Do you remember what this street smelled like in the old days?

FARID
Kabob.

AMIR
Lamb kabob.

FARID
(tasting the word)
Lamb kabob.

A red Toyota pickup truck cruises slowly down the street. A handful of stern-faced YOUNG TALIBS sit in the truck's bed, Kalashnikovs slung over their shoulders. They all wear beards and black turbans.

FARID
Beard patrol.

One TALIB'S roaming eyes fall on Amir. Amir holds his gaze.

The truck rolls away.

FARID
(hissing)

What's the matter with you?

AMIR
What?

FARID
Don't you ever stare at them! Understand me? Never!

Farid stalks away. Amir, chastened, follows. Briefly hearing echoes of the happy kite running day from his past.

EXT. ORPHANAGE – DAY

The barracks-style building stands by the banks of the dried-up Kabul River, its windows boarded over with wood planks.

Amir and Farid walk from the Land Cruiser to the door of the orphanage. CHILDREN run inside.

Int. Orphanage – Day

The children scatter amongst their squalid blankets. Amir and Farid enter. After a few seconds, ZAMAN, a man with a shaggy black beard, tentatively greets them.

ZAMAN
Salaam alaykum.

AMIR
Salaam alaykum.

He pulls the Polaroid of Hassan and Sohrab out of his pocket and shows it to Zaman.

AMIR
We're looking for this boy.

Zaman gives the photo a cursory glance.

ZAMAN
I'm sorry. I've never seen him.

FARID
You barely looked at the picture, my friend.

Zaman sighs and takes the photo from Amir's hand. He studies it before handing it back to Amir.

ZAMAN
I know all the children here and that one doesn't look familiar. And now, if you'll permit me. . .

AMIR
Agha! Agha, we don't mean him any harm.

ZAMAN (O.S.)
I told you he's not here. Now please, go away.

FARID
Friend, we are not with the Taliban. The man who is with me wants to take this boy to a safe place.

AMIR
I knew Sohrab's father. His name was Hassan. There's hope for this boy, Agha. A way out. I can take him back to America with me.
  (*beat*)
I'm his uncle.

A moment passes.

Int. Director's Office - Moments Later

Amir and Farid follow Zaman through dim, grimy hallways to a decrepit back room with a table and chairs.

ZAMAN
What I have to tell you is not pleasant. I tell you because I believe you. You have the look of desperate men.

Amir and Farid sit on folding chairs across a worn desk from Zaman.

Zaman's gaze lingers for a moment.

ZAMAN
There is a Talib official. He visits every month or two. He brings cash with him— not a lot, but better than nothing. Usually he takes a girl. But not always.

For a few seconds Amir and Farid are silent, processing this.

AMIR
And you allow this?

ZAMAN
What choice do I have?

AMIR
You're the director here. Your job is to watch over these children.

ZAMAN
There's nothing I can do.

Amir rises from his chair, face darkening with anger.

AMIR
You're selling children!

Farid stands and takes Amir's arm.

FARID
Easy—

AMIR
You're here to protect them!

ZAMAN
Yes, I am here to protect them.

He stands, hands on the desk, and stares back at Amir.

FARID
Sit.

Amir calms down and sits.

ZAMAN
And you, brother? You come here to rescue a boy, take him back to America, give him a good life. It must seem heroic, huh? But what of the other two hundred children?

You'll never see them again. You'll never hear them howling in the night.

Fury growing, Zalman points a finger at Amir, who spies SMALL BOYS crouched in the doorway, peering into the room.

ZAMAN
I spent my life savings on this orphanage. Everything I ever owned or inherited I sold to run this godforsaken place. You think I don't have family in Pakistan or Iran? I could have run like everyone else.

Zaman leans toward Amir, whose gaze is fixed to the table.

ZAMAN
If I deny him one child, he takes ten. So I

let him take one and leave the judging to Allah. I take his filthy money and I go to the bazaar and I buy food for the children. You think I spend it on myself?
(indicating his shabby appearance)
Look at me. *Look!*

FARID
What happens to the children he takes?

ZAMAN
Sometimes they come back. More often they don't.

AMIR
Who is he? How do I find him?

ZAMAN
Go to Ghazi Stadium tomorrow. You'll see

him at halftime. He'll be the one making speeches.

He sits wearily, as if it pains his knees to bend them.

ZAMAN
Now please leave. You've frightened the children.

EXT. WAZIR AKBAR KHAN DISTRICT – LATER

The Land Cruiser rolls down the street familiar to us from Amir's childhood. Unlike the rest of Kabul, this neighborhood still looks fairly well-maintained.

INT. LAND CRUISER – CONTINUOUS

Amir stares at the familiar sights.

AMIR
Stop the car.

EXT. BABA'S HOUSE – CONTINUOUS

Amir pulls open the rusted iron gate and walks up the driveway leading to his father's house.

The poplar trees have been chopped down. The lawn is nothing but brown dirt now. A car is parked where Baba's Mustang used to sit. Oil has spilled onto the driveway, staining it.

The house is a pale remnant of its former glory. The roof sags and the plaster is cracked. Many of the windows are broken and patched with sheets of clear plastic.

INT. CAR – CONTINUOUS

FARID
(calling out the window)
We should go.

EXT. BABA'S HOUSE – CONTINUOUS

Amir stares up at the broken house for one last moment.

INT. CAR – MOMENTS LATER

Amir stands at the open passenger door.

AMIR
I have to look at one more thing.

FARID
Nothing that you remember has survived. Better to forget.

AMIR
I don't want to forget anymore.

Amir shuts the door.

Ext. Cemetery – Sunset

Amir climbs to the top of the hill and enters the abandoned graveyard. The headstones are barely visible through the thick tangles of weeds.

The pomegranate tree has been chopped down. Amir hunkers down on his knees and inspects the stump.

After a moment he finds what he's looking for. The carving is faded but still legible: "Amir and Hassan, the Sultans of Kabul." He traces the curves of each letter with his fingers.

EXT. GHAZI STADIUM – DAY

Amir and Farid sit amongst thousands of spectators on the concrete terraces overlooking the soccer pitch.

The playing field is nothing but pitted dirt. A pair of deep holes plunge into the soil behind the south-end goalposts.

A whistle blows, signalling halftime. The players jog off the field. They are all bearded and wear shorts.

Young, gun-toting TALIBS roam the aisles, striking anyone who cheers too loudly.

A pair of dusty pickup trucks drives into the stadium. A woman in a Pink burqa sits in the back of one of the trucks; a blindfolded man sits in the other.

A tall, broad-shouldered TALIB IN WHITE stands in the first truck. His sparkling white garment glimmers in the afternoon sun. He wears dark, round sunglasses like the ones John Lennon wore.

The crowd rises to its feet, watching the trucks ride around the track that circles the field.

The trucks drive onto the playing field and stop behind the south-end goalposts. A third truck meets them there. This truck's bed is loaded down with rocks.

FARID

Do you want to stay here?

AMIR

No. But we have to.

Two TALIBS with AK-47s slung over their shoulders help the blindfolded man from the back of the first truck. Two others help the burqa-clad woman. The captives' arms are bound.

The woman's knees buckle and she slumps to the ground. The soldiers pull her up and she screams. It is the cry of a wild animal trying to pry its mangled leg from the trap.

Two more Talibs help their comrades, forcing the woman to the ground as she struggles.

A black-bearded CHUBBY CLERIC dressed in gray garments stands at midfield. He clears his throat into a handheld microphone. Behind him the woman still screams.

The cleric speaks with a commanding baritone that rings out from the stadium's speakers.

> **CLERIC**
> Brothers and sisters! We are here today to carry out Shari'a. We are here today to carry out justice. We listen to what God says and we obey! And what does God say? I ask you? WHAT DOES GOD SAY? God says that every sinner must be punished in a manner befitting his sin. Those are not my words, nor the words of my brothers. Those are the words of GOD!

He points with his free hand to the sky.

> **CLERIC**
> And what manner of punishment befits the adulterer? How shall we punish those who dishonor the sanctity of marriage? How shall we deal with those who disobey God? How shall we answer those who throw stones at the windows of God's house? WE SHALL THROW THE STONES BACK.

He shuts off the microphone. A low-pitched murmur spreads through the crowd.

The TALIB IN WHITE selects a stone the size of a baseball from the truck bed. He shows it to the crowd. Like a pitcher on the mound, he hurls the stone at the blindfolded man, hitting the man's head with a sickening thunk.

The crowd makes a startled "OH!" sound. Blood begins to stain the pink burqa. More Talibs pick up rocks and begin stoning the doomed couple. None are as athletic as the Talib in White; the others throw their stones from far closer range.

Amir closes his eyes and covers his face with his hands. The spectators' "OH!" follows each crack of stone on flesh. And the doomed woman's wail rises above all other noise.

EXT. GHAZI STADIUM – LATER

WORKERS dump the bloodied corpses into the back of one of the trucks. One of them tries to cover a large bloodstain by kicking dirt over it.

Amir and Farid approach a gun-carrying Talib on the field.

> **FARID**
> My friend? My friend. A word?

The Talib glances at Farid.

> **FARID**
> *(gesturing to the field)*
> We have business with your brother.

He rubs his fingers together, the international symbol for money.

> **FARID**
> Personal business.

The Talib nods and approaches the chubby cleric, who is chatting with some comrades on the sidelines.

The young man addresses the cleric, who listens and glances at Farid and Amir. The Talib in White turns to look at them, too. His gaze fixes on Amir.

EXT. TALIB COMPOUND – DAY

The Land Cruiser eases into the driveway of a big house shaded by tall willows—some of the only trees in Kabul.

INT. LAND CRUISER – CONTINUOUS

Farid kills the engine and for a moment there is quiet, broken only by the tink-tink of the engine cooling. Farid shifts in his seat and toys with the keys hanging from the ignition switch. He doesn't look at Amir.

> **FARID**
> *(apologetic)*
> I guess I'll wait in the car. This is your business now.

Amir grips the man's shoulder.

> **AMIR**
> Thank you for helping me.

EXT. MANSION – DAY

Amir comes to a small metal gate in the outer wall of the compound.

> **AMIR**
> *Salaam alaykum.* Anyone there?

A TALIB GUARD approaches.

> **AMIR**
> I was told to come here.

A moment later the guard unlocks the gate.

> **TALIB GUARD**
> Come in.

> **AMIR**
> Thank you.

The gate is locked behind him.

A group of TALIB GUARDS toting AK-47s stare at Amir.

The armed men frisk him from head to toe, patting his legs, feeling his crotch. One comments to the other in Pashtu.

> **TALIB GUARD**
> How soft.

They all laugh. They gesture for Amir to follow.

INT. MANSION – DAY

They enter the sparsely-furnished house.

Int. Sitting Room - Day

The guards lead Amir into a room with twin black sofas.

TALIB GUARD
Sit down.

The older of the two guards motions to one of the sofas with the barrel of his gun. Amir sits and the guards leave.

Amir stares at the coffee table in front of him.

The door opens and the armed men return. The Talib in White stands between them, still wearing his John Lennon sunglasses, looking like a broad-shouldered mystic.

Amir stands to greet him.

AMIR
Salaam alaykum.
  (beat)
I think there's been a mistake. I came to see your friend.

The Talib in white says nothing, staring at Amir.

AMIR
The man who made the speech at the stadium.

TALIB IN WHITE
He has other business.
  (beat)
You can do away with that now.

AMIR
I'm not sure what you mean.

TALIB IN WHITE
Take off your beard.

Amir reluctantly removes his false beard.

TALIB IN WHITE
One of the better ones I've seen.

Amir's cheeks are red from the sting of the plucked-off beard. His eyes flick from the guards'

Kalashnikovs to the Talib in White.

TALIB IN WHITE
Take off the turban.

Amir does.

TALIB IN WHITE
You come from America?

AMIR
Yes. I'm looking for a boy.

TALIB IN WHITE
Isn't everybody?

AMIR
I understand your friend brought him here. His name is Sohrab.

TALIB IN WHITE
Let me ask you something: What are you doing with that whore America? Why aren't you here, with your Muslim brothers, serving your country?

Amir hesitates, searching for an inoffensive answer.

AMIR
I've been away for a long time.

The Talib turns to his guards.

TALIB IN WHITE
That's an answer?

GUARD #1
No, Agha sahib.

GUARD #2
No, Agha sahib.

The Talib turns back to Amir and shrugs.

TALIB IN WHITE
Not an answer, they say.

The Talib sits on a sofa.

AMIR
I'm only here for the boy.

TALIB IN WHITE
Do you want to see him?

AMIR
Yes.

Int. Sitting Room – Moments Later

We hear footfalls, and the jingle of bells with each step.

A guard returns, carrying a boombox stereo. Behind him, a boy dressed in a loose, blue *pirhan-tumban* follows.

SOHRAB looks uncannily similar to his father at that age. His head is shaved, his eyes darkened with mascara, his cheeks glowing with rouge.

When he stops in the middle of the room, the bells strapped around his anklets stop jingling. His eyes linger on Amir for a moment. Then he looks down at his own naked feet.

The guard with the boombox presses play and Pashtu music fills the room. The two guards begin to clap.

Sohrab raises his arms and turns slowly. He stands on tiptoes, spins gracefully, dips to his knees, straightens, and spins again. His little hands swivel at the wrists, his fingers snap, his head swings side to side like a pendulum.

His feet pound the floor, the bells jingling in perfect harmony with the beat of the tabla. He keeps his eyes closed.

Sohrab dances until the Talib stops the music.

TALIB IN WHITE
Come, my boy.

He beckons for Sohrab and the boy walks to him, head down, and sits next to the man. The Talib wraps his arm around the boy.

TALIB IN WHITE
Such a talented little Hazara!
  (to guards)
Leave us be.

The guards exit.

TALIB IN WHITE
I've been wondering. . . Whatever happened to your great Baba, anyway?

The question hits Amir like a physical blow.

TALIB IN WHITE
What did you think? That you'd put on a fake beard and I wouldn't recognize you? I knew you the second I saw you in the stadium. I never forget a face. Not ever.

AMIR
Assef.

TALIB IN WHITE/ASSEF
Amir jan.

AMIR
What are you doing here?

ASSEF
Me? I'm home. The question is, what are *you* doing here?

Amir lowers his eyes. For a long count he stares at the floor. Finally he raises his head and looks at Assef.

AMIR
I'm taking the boy home with me.

Neither man blinks.

ASSEF
You want my advice? Run away. That's what you do best.

AMIR

Not without Sohrab.

ASSEF

Why's that? The boy's too good for his country? What do you know about Afghanistan? You weren't here when the Communists shot our mullahs and pissed in our mosques. This country was like a beautiful mansion littered with garbage. We took out the garbage. We brought law. We brought justice.

AMIR

I have seen your laws. . . and your justice. And I'm taking the boy home with me.

ASSEF

All right, then.

He shoves Sohrab, knocking the boy into Amir.

Amir stands, helping Sohrab to his feet. He takes the boy's hand and the boy stares up at him.

Assef removes his turban, loosing curls of shoulder length hair. He presses play on the boombox and turns the volume all the way up.

ASSEF

Of course, I didn't say you could take him for free.

He grins at Amir and, without further warning,

hits him hard in the jaw.

Amir struggles to his feet, blood already spilling from his mouth. Assef throws him against a wall and a framed picture shatters and falls to the floor.

Amir tries to fight but he doesn't know how. Assef smashes him in the mouth, dropping Amir again.

As Amir struggles to rise Assef grabs his hair and punches him in the nose. Amir crawls across the floor, blood from his torn lips staining the carpet.

Pashtu music plays at deafening volume.

Assef lifts him and throws him against the wall again, with so much power that hairline cracks open up in the plaster.

Assef tackles Amir and they crash through the wooden coffee table, setting brass ball studs rolling.

Assef kicks Amir again and again. Blood leaks from Amir's nostrils, from his lips, from a gash that splits his forehead. The music stops.

Assef grabs a chair to finish Amir off, but as he turns to smash it, he sees the young boy.

Sohrab holds a Fly Bye slingshot in his hands, the same slingshot Amir gave to Hassan years before.

The cup at the end of the elastic band, pulled all the way back, cradles one of the brass balls from the coffee table.

SOHRAB
No more. No more, Agha. Please stop hurting him.

Amir blinks the blood from his eyes, staring at the boy. The slingshot is aimed at Assef's face.

ASSEF
Put it down, Hazara. You'll get yours next.

SOHRAB
Please, Agha. Please stop.

ASSEF
Put it down.

Assef lunges at Sohrab. The slingshot makes a *thwiiiit* sound when Sohrab releases the cup. Assef screams. He puts his hand where his left eye had been a moment ago. Blood and vitreous fluid, white and gel-like, oozes between his fingers.

He falls to the carpet, rolling side to side, shrieking, hand still cupped over the bloody socket.

Sohrab grabs Amir's hand and helps him to his feet.

ASSEF
OUT! GET IT OUT!

Sohrab leads Amir to the window and opens it. They climb out.

INT. OUTER ROOM – DAY

The guards play backgammon in the outer room. Their own radio has drowned out most of the violence, but now Assef's shrieks become audible.

They grab their rifles and run for the sitting room.

EXT. BACK OF BUILDING – DAY

Sohrab guides Amir down the narrow walkway between the back of the building and the compound wall. They climb over the wall.

INT. SITTING ROOM – DAY

The two guards huddle over the shrieking Assef.

The older guard, tending to his maimed leader, gestures to the younger guard, who stands and hurries out.

ASSEF
Kill him!

EXT. TALIB COMPOUND – DAY

Amir's arm is around Sohrab's shoulder, the boy keeping Amir upright. They run for freedom.

Farid jumps out of the Land Cruiser, runs over to him, and slings Amir's arm around his shoulders.

Sohrab runs alongside them. Farid hurries Amir to the car and into the backseat; Sohrab gets into the backseat with him.

The young guard runs out of the mansion. He spots the interlopers trying to make a getaway. He raises his AK-47 and fires a burst of bullets.

Farid jumps into the driver's seat, turns the ignition, and hits the gas, the wheels spinning in the dusty driveway for a second before finding traction. They speed away.

Bullets shatter the Land Cruiser's windows and perforate the steel panels.

EXT. BACK ROADS OF AFGHANISTAN – DUSK

The Land Cruiser, avoiding the major roads, navigates along rocky back roads little wider than goat paths.

Ext. Border Crossing – Day

A road sign says *Welcome to Pakistan* in Pashtu, Farsi, and English. The Land Cruiser pulls up to a gate arm blocking the road. A PAKISTANI SOLDIER approaches the car.

Production design by Carlos Conti; graphic illustration by Maud Gircourt.

Farid opens the window and hands the soldier a folded hundred dollar greenback. The soldier glances at the battered man sitting beside the quiet boy in the backseat.

The soldier considers this tableau for a moment before waving them through.

EXT. RAHIM KHAN'S BUILDING – NIGHT

The Land Cruiser is parked by the curb. Farid stands with Amir and Sohrab by the building's front door. Amir's face is badly bruised but he's able to stand on his own.

> **AMIR**
> Go home to your family.

Farid hugs Amir goodbye.

INT. RAHIM KHAN'S APARTMENT – NIGHT

Amir knocks on the door. No answer. He knocks again.

An ELDERLY NEIGHBOR across the hallway opens her door and peers at Amir and Sohrab.

> **NEIGHBOR**
> Are you Amir?

> **AMIR**
> Yes.

The neighbor hands Amir a manila envelope and a key.

> **NEIGHBOR**
> Rahim Khan left this for you.

Amir accepts the envelope and key.

> **AMIR**
> Where did he go?

The neighbor gives a philosophical shrug.

> **NEIGHBOR**
> I did not ask.

> **AMIR**
> But he'll be back?

NEIGHBOR
He has left us, my child.

INT. RAHIM KHAN'S APARTMENT – MOMENTS LATER

Amir and Sohrab step inside. The place has been emptied. No furniture (save for a mattress on the floor), no clothes, no sign that anyone ever lived here.

Int. Rahim Khan's Apartment - Later

Amir has washed the blood off his battered face and wrapped a bandage around his forehead. He sits on the mattress, back against the wall, dealing out five cards for himself and five for his opponent, though he has no opponent.

Sohrab, also cleaned up, stands at the window looking down at the street.

AMIR
You're wasting your hand.

Sohrab doesn't answer.

INT. RAHIM KHAN'S APARTMENT – MORNING

Amir wakes up on his mat in the corner of the apartment.

AMIR
Sohrab?

Amir sees that the mat Sohrab had been lying on is now empty. He looks around the apartment, panicking.

EXT. STREETS OF PESHAWAR – DAY

Amir hurries down the street, dodging WOMEN IN BURKAS, YOUNG BOYS chasing a hairless dog, and BLIND PANHANDLERS. He looks down every alleyway he passes, looks inside store

fronts, asks a man selling newspapers if he's seen a Hazara boy.

Sohrab is gone.

Amir runs through the streets of the strange city, sweating through his shirt.

The sun beats down on the crowded, dirty city. The locals shelter from the heat in the shade but Amir never stops.

PAKISTANIS and AFGHAN EXILES stare with suspicion at this foreigner with the desperate face.

In the distance he spots a BOY dressed like Sohrab and follows after him.

Ext. Mosque of Mahabat Khan – Day

The boy enters the mosque.

Amir follows them.

INT. MOSQUE – DAY

It's here that the boy sits with his FATHER. It is not Sohrab. Amir bends over to catch his breath. He's distracted, seems out of place in the mosque.

> **SMILING MAN**
> Take off your shoes, dear brother.

AMIR

Forgive me.

INT. MOSQUE OF MAHABAT KHAN – MOMENTS LATER

Shoeless, Amir cleanses his bare feet.

INT. MOSQUE OF MAHABAT KHAN – LATER

Amir kneels in the main prayer hall. He takes a deep breath and lowers his forehead to the ground.

Tears spill from his eyes as Amir bows to the west.

AMIR

La illaha il Allah, Muhammad u rasul ullah.

There is no God but Allah and Muhammad is His messenger.

EXT. MOSQUE OF MAHABAT KHAN – DAY

Amir walks out of the mosque, amongst his fellow worshippers. His search has failed. He trudges away, defeated.

EXT. RAHIM KHAN'S BUILDING – DAY

Amir walks down the street, despondent. He turns the corner onto Rahim Khan's street. A half a block from the building, Amir sees the small boy sitting on the steps.

For a moment, he cannot believe it. He sits down next to him.

AMIR

I thought I lost you.

Sohrab stares at the minaret. For a long time he is quiet.

SOHRAB

He used to come get me in the morning, before prayers.
    (beat)
I didn't want him to get me anymore.

AMIR

He won't, Sohrab. I swear to you, he can't get you anymore.

SOHRAB

Are your parents dead?

AMIR

Yes.

SOHRAB

Do you remember what they look like?

AMIR

I never met my mother. I remember what my father looked like.

Sohrab remains motionless.

SOHRAB

I'm starting to forget their faces. Is that bad?

Amir hesitates. He pulls the Polaroid from his pants pocket and hands it to Sohrab.

AMIR

Here.

It's the picture of Hassan and Sohrab standing outside the gates of Baba's old house. Sohrab holds the photo in both hands, tracing his thumb over its surface.

SOHRAB

Sometimes I'm glad they're dead.

AMIR

Why?

SOHRAB

Because—because I don't want them to see me. I'm so dirty.

Amir touches his arm but Sohrab flinches.

AMIR

You're not dirty.

Amir reaches again, gently.

AMIR

I won't hurt you.

Amir wraps his arms around Sohrab's limp body.

INT. AIRPORT – DAY

Soraya stands with a group of PAKISTANI-AMERICANS waiting for their loved ones outside of customs.

She searches through dozens of unfamiliar faces, smiling PAKISTANIS greeting their loved ones.

Finally Amir and Sohrab step through the doors. Sohrab wears a long-sleeve T-shirt and blue jeans.

>**AMIR**
>That's my wife.

Soraya locks her arms around Amir's neck. He closes his eyes, face buried in her thick black hair.

>**AMIR**
>I missed you.

>**SORAYA**
>I missed you too.

She releases him and kneels to eye level with Sohrab. She takes the boy's hand and smiles at him.

>**AMIR**
>Sohrab jan. This is your aunt.

>**SORAYA**
>*Salaam*, Sohrab jan. We've all been waiting for you. Ready to meet your new family? Let's go.

Sohrab shifts on his feet and looks away. Soraya glances at Amir, who shrugs and nods: give it time.

Int. Amir's Apartment, Guest Room – Night

Soraya has spent days preparing the apartment for Sohrab's arrival, converting the guest room into a child's bedroom.

Soraya, Amir and Sohrab stand by the door.

>**SORAYA**
>(*to Sohrab*)
>Do you like your new room?

Sohrab lowers his head. He walks over to the bed and lies down, facing away from Amir and Soraya.

INT. AMIR'S APARTMENT, HALLWAY – MOMENTS LATER

Amir finds Soraya staring into the mirror in the bathroom. He smiles.

>**SORAYA**
>You don't look so bad.
>(*beat*)
>I don't think he's looked at me once.

>**AMIR**
>Give him time.

**INT. AMIR'S APARTMENT, DINING ROOM –
LATER**

Amir, Soraya, General Taheri, and the General's wife Jamila sit around the table, passing heaping platters of lamb and spinach, meatballs and chick peas, and orange rice.

A fifth place setting goes unused, the fifth chair conspicuously empty.

JAMILA
I'm knitting him a turtleneck sweater for next winter. The sweaters they sell here don't last a month.

The general sips his wine and sets the glass down.

GENERAL TAHERI
Amir jan, you're going to tell me why you've brought this boy back with you?

JAMILA
Iqbal jan! What sort of question is that?

GENERAL TAHERI
While you're busy knitting sweaters, my dear, I have to deal with the community's perception of our family. People will ask. They will want to know why there is a Hazara boy living with our daughter. What do I tell them?

Soraya drops her fork and turns on her father.

SORAYA
You can tell them—

AMIR
It's alright. The General is correct. People will ask.

SORAYA
Amir—

AMIR
It's all right.
  (to the general)
You see, General Sahib, my father slept

with his servant's wife. She bore him a son named Hassan. Hassan is dead now. That boy sleeping in the other room is Hassan's son. He's my nephew. That's what you tell people when they ask.

Everyone stares at Amir.

AMIR
And one more thing, General Sahib. You will never again refer to him as a "Hazara boy" in my presence. He has a name and it's Sohrab.

Amir resumes his meal. His in-laws sit quietly, stunned by his words and demeanor. Soraya can't quite hide her smile.

Ext. Lake Elizabeth Park – Day

A strong breeze blows through the park, ruffling the kites flying high above.

AFGHAN FAMILIES gather in one corner of the park, standing by grills loaded with *morgh* kabob.

CHILDREN kick a soccer ball and scream at each other.

Sohrab stands alone, farther up the sloping hill, wearing a black and blue raincoat.

Amir speaks with an AFGHAN-AMERICAN DOCTOR. Soraya walks over to them and pulls on Amir's sleeve.

SORAYA
Amir jan, look!

She's pointing to the sky. Six kites fly high, speckles of bright yellow, red, and green against the gray sky.

AMIR
  (to the doctor)
Excuse me a second.

Amir walks over to a KITE SELLER, another Afghan, at a nearby stand.

AMIR
Salaam. I'd like that kite please. And I'll take this spool.

The kite seller turns to get the kite as Amir tests the cut of the glass line.

EXT. LAKE ELIZABETH PARK – MOMENTS LATER

Amir approaches Sohrab, who stands with his arms at his sides, staring at the sky.

AMIR
Do you like the kite?

Sohrab's eyes shift from the sky to the kite and back.

Twenty yards away, Soraya, watches Amir and Sohrab.

AMIR
Did I ever tell you your father was the best kite runner in Kabul?

Amir knots the loose end of the spool wire to the string loop tied to the central spar.

AMIR
He made all the neighborhood kids jealous. He'd run kites and never look up at the sky. Some claimed he was just chasing the kite's shadow. But they didn't know him like I did. Your father wasn't chasing shadows. He just knew. That's all.

Another half-dozen kites have taken flight. People gather in small groups, teacups in hand, gazing into the sky.

AMIR
Do you want to help me fly this?

Sohrab's gaze bounces from the kite to Amir to the sky.

AMIR
Okay. Looks like I'll have to fly it solo.

Amir balances the spool in his left hand and feeds about three feet of line. The yellow kite dangles above the grass.

AMIR
Last chance.

Sohrab watches Amir prepare for flight.

AMIR
All right. Here I go.

The kite lifts, soaring into the sky as Amir lets the spool spin in his left hand and guides the string with his right.

AMIR
It's a good kite, no?

For a moment Amir proudly watches his flying kite. When he looks down, he sees Sohrab standing beside him, motionless.

AMIR
Do you want to try?

Sohrab says nothing.

AMIR
Here.

When Amir holds the string out for him, the boy's hand finally reaches out. He hesitates and takes the string.

Amir spins the spool to gather the loose line. He turns and sees Soraya watching them.

SORAYA
Hold it tight, Sohrab jan.

AMIR
Good job, Sohrab.

In the sky, a green kite closes in on Amir's yellow flyer. Amir traces the green kite's glass wire to a CREWCUT KID thirty yards away. The Kid sees Amir looking at him.

AMIR

Looks like someone wants to fight.

Sohrab hands the string back to Amir.

AMIR

Are you sure?

Sohrab takes the spool. Amir grins. The boy knows how this game is played.

AMIR

Let's teach him a lesson, no?

Sohrab's gaze flits from their yellow kite to the Crewcut Kid's green one. His eyes are suddenly alert.

AMIR

Watch, Sohrab. I'm going to show you one of your father's favorite tricks. An old tech-nique. Lift and Dive.

The spool rolls in Sohrab's palms. The green kite hovers above the yellow one, holds its position for a moment and then shoots down.

AMIR

Come closer. Here he comes!

Amir loosens his grip and tugs on the string, dip-ping and dodging the green kite. A series of quick sidearm jerks and the yellow kite soars up coun-ter-clockwise, in a half circle.

AMIR

We're going to catch him now, right?

The green kite scrambles, panic-stricken. Amir pulls hard on the line, forcing the yellow kite to plummet, its glass wire slicing the green kite's wire.

The green kite spins out of control.

AMIR
Look, I cut him!

The crew-cut boy turns on his young spooler.

CREW CUT BOY
What are you doing? You can't hold it right?

Amir, panting and exhilarated, looks down at Sohrab. One corner of the boy's mouth has curled up in a lopsided smile.

AMIR
Do you want me to run that kite for you?

Sohrab's Adam's apple rises and falls as he swallows. He nods, a very slight nod but a nod all the same.

AMIR
For you, a thousand times over.

Amir runs, a grown man running like a child over the hill. The wind blows in his face and he runs, a smile as wide as the Valley of Panjsher on his lips.

Behind him, Sohrab slowly climbs the hill and watches. The sky behind him is clear and blue, scattered with kites.

The End

For you, a thousand times over.

DREAMWORKS PICTURES
SIDNEY KIMMEL ENTERTAINMENT
and
PARTICIPANT PRODUCTIONS
Present
A
SIDNEY KIMMEL ENTERTAINMENT
and
PARKES/MacDONALD
Production

A MARC FORSTER Film

The Kite Runner

KHALID ABDALLA
HOMAYOUN ERSHADI
SHAUN TOUB
ATOSSA LEONI
SAÏD TAGHMAOUI
and Introducing
ZEKIRIA EBRAHIMI
ALI DANISH BAKHTYARI
AHMAD KHAN MAHMOODZADA

Casting by
KATE DOWD

Music by
ALBERTO IGLESIAS

Co-Executive Producer
BRUCE TOLL

Costume Designer
FRANK FLEMING

Edited by
MATT CHESSÉ, A.C.E.

Production Designer
CARLOS CONTI

Director of Photography
ROBERTO SCHAEFER, ASC

Executive Producers
SIDNEY KIMMEL
LAURIE MacDONALD
SAM MENDES
JEFF SKOLL

Produced by
WILLIAM HORBERG
WALTER PARKES

Produced by
REBECCA YELDHAM
E. BENNETT WALSH

Based Upon the Book by
KHALED HOSSEINI

Screenplay by
DAVID BENIOFF

Directed by
MARC FORSTER

CAST

Amir	KHALID ABDALLA
Soraya	ATOSSA LEONI
Rahim Khan	SHAUN TOUB
Omar	SAYED JAFAR MASIHULLAH GHARIBZADA
Young Amir	ZEKIRIA EBRAHIMI
Young Hassan	AHMAD KHAN MAHMOODZADA
Business Man in Baba's Study	MIR MAHMOOD SHAH HASHIMI
Baba	HOMAYOUN ERSHADI
Ali	NABI TANHA
Young Assef	ELHAM EHSAS
Wali	BAHRAM EHSAS
Kamal	TAMIM NAWABI
Uncle Saifo the Kite Seller	MOHAMAD NABI ATTAI
Spice Merchant	MOHAMAD NADIR SARWARI
Party Worker	MUSTAFA HAIDARI
Birthday Singer	AHMAD YASAR SHIR AGHA
Mahmood	MOHAMMAD AMAN JOYA
Karim	ABDUL AZIM WAHABZADA
Soviet Union Soldier	VSEVOLOD SEVANCHOS
Burly Man in Truck	SAYED MIRAN FARHAD
Young Wife in Truck	MURINA ABUDUKELIMU
Soviet Union Officer	IGOR RADCHENKO
Gas Station Customer	LARRY BROWN
Dean of Students	L. PETER CALLENDER
Man at Bar	JESSE ROBERTSON
Pool Players	JOSH CHAMBERLAIN MARCO MAZARIEGOS, SHAAN PRICE
General Taheri	QADIR FAROOKH
Flea Market Customer	PEG McKIBBIN
Dr. Starobin	CHRIS VERRILL
Dr. Amani	AMAR KUREISHI
Jamila Taheri	MAIMOONA GHIZAL
Wedding Singer	MOHAMMAD EHSAN AMAN
Cemetery Mullah	YUNUS OSMAN
Pakistan Taxi Driver	MEHBOOB ALI
Farid	SAÏD TAGHMAOUI
Zaman the Orphanage Director	NASSER MEMARZIA
Assef	ABDUL SALAM YUSOUFZAI
Taliban Stadium Speaker	MOHAMAD AMIN RAHIMI
Assef Guards	AZIZ RAXIDI, KHALIL AHMAD NOORYAN

Sohrab . . . . ALI DANISH BAKHTYARI
Rahim Khan's Neighbor . . . . HAMEEDA HAMRAZ
Man at Mosque . . . . .KAISER DOULAT-BEEK
Man in the Park . . . . AHMAD SHAH ALAM
Doctor in the Park . . . . KHALED HOSSEINI
Park Kite Seller . . . . HABIB ZARGI
Kite Flyer Kid . . . . HOUSHMAND HABIB
Kite Spooler Kid . . . . LUKAS FERREIRA
Stunt Coordinator. . . . . WANG HAI
Stunts . . . . .LU JIN CHAO, NING JUN

CREW

Unit Production Manager. . . . . E. BENNETT WALSH
First Assistant Director . . . . MICHAEL LERMAN
Second Assistant Director . . . . PETER THORELL
Associate Producers. . . . KWAME L. PARKER, LESLIE McMINN
Visual Effects Supervisor. . . . . KEVIN TOD HAUG
Art Director . . . . KAREN MURPHY
Set Decorators . . . . CAROLINE SMITH, MARIA NAY
Camera/Steadicam Operator . . . . JIM McCONKEY
First Assistant Photographer . . . . .ZORAN VESELIC
Still Photographer . . . . .PHIL BRAY
Script Supervisor . . . . .MASSOUMEH EMAMI
Production Sound Mixer . . . . CHRIS MUNRO
Chief Lighting Technician . . . . IAN R. KINCAID
Key Grip. . . . . HERBERT LEE AULT
Costume Supervisor. . . . . SUSAN J. WRIGHT
Makeup Department Head . . . . .KRISTINA VOGEL
Key Hair Stylist . . . . .TERESA MAREE HINTON
Production Coordinator . . . . DAMIANA KAMISHIN
Production Accountant. . . . . TISH JOHNSON
Production Liaison. . . . . S. DYLAN KIRKLAND
Afghan Cast Interpreter . . . . .ILHAM HOSSEINI
Supervising Location Manager . . . . DOUGLAS DRESSER
Unit Publicist . . . . BLAISE J. NOTO
Transportation Coordinator / Unit Manager . . . . . . HENRY DRAY
Transportation Coordinator . . . . DEREK RASER
Casting Executive. .LESLEE FELDMAN
Assistant to Mr. Forster . . . . JILLIAN KUGLER
Assistant to Mr. Horberg . . . . CHANTAL NONG
Assistant to Mr. Parkes. . . . . .RIYOKO TANAKA
Assistant to Ms. Yeldham. . . . . LAUREN McCLARD
Los Angeles Office Assistant . . . . ADAM BAYLESS

CHINA UNIT

Production Supervisor China. . . . . HUANG FAN "NINA"
First Assistant Director . . . . .ZHANG JIN ZHAN
Second Assistant Director . . . . .QIAO HEPIN
Assistant Production Manager. . . . . ADA SHEN
Xinjiang Production Manager . . . . AKBAR YIMING
Art Director . . . . .OLEH SOKOLOVSKY
On-Set Props ROBERT "MOXY" MOXHAM, RICHARD CROWE
Assistant Art Directors . . . MICHAEL TURNER, XIN YAN RONG

A Second Assistant Photographer . . . . LEE JAKE MARIANO
B Camera Operator . . . . LAM FAI TAI
B First Assistant Photographer. . . . . BRETT MATTHEWS
B Second Assistant Photographer . . . . LESLEY WATSON
Film Loader . . . . .ROWENA MOLLICA
Camera Department Translator . . . . .ABDUKADER MAMAT
Boom Operator. . . . . STEPHEN FINN
Utility Sound . . . . YANG FAN
Video Assist . . . . .MICHAEL TAYLOR
Assistant Video Assist . . . . .ZECHARIAH KATZ
Chief Lighting Technician . . . . .KANG XIAO TIAN
Assistant Chief Lighting Technicians . . . . . . .MARK HADLAND
CAO XUE ZHONG, WANG JUN XI
Lighting Technicians . . . . . . .SUN BING RUI, SUN CHEN YANG,
SUN GEN SHANG, LI SI GUANG, ZHANG TAO,
CAO ZHONG XUE, CAO YONG JIE,
LI CONG LI, CAO WEI DONG
Chief Rigging Technician . . . . KIM K. KONO
Second Company Grip. DUSTIN AULT
Dolly Grip . . . . .TIM CHRISTIE
Grips. SANLANG, SUN HONG YANG,
CAO WU TONG, XIN HONG BIN, SUN JUN YANG,
KANG HAI LIANG, CHEN KAI, LIU YANG, ZHANG
QUAN, BIA HONG QUN, MAO WAI QIN, SI XUE WEN
Translator. . . . . QI ZI YIN "FIONA"
Rigging Key Grip. SKYLER TEGLAND
Property Master . . . . SUE BOWCOTT
Property Buyer. . . . . LI MING SHAN
Assistant Property Master . . . . HOU YI
China Casting. .ERIKO MIYAGAWA
Background Casting. . . . . .FANG DAN RUI "ZOE"
Xinjiang Background Casting . . . . XIRELI ABUDUREXITI
MARIDEL AISAM, ABLIZ ABDIRIXIT
MUHAMD ALI, YUKESAIKE XIJAET
AKEMUSULITAN SULAIMANXIA,
DALI MAITUXIA, NIYAT ULLAH BAIG
Beijing Background Casting . . . . MO LAN
Dari Language Teachers. .SALAH YAFTALI, MASOUD FARAND
Kite Master. . . . . .BASIR BERIA
Armourer . . . . YU XIAO MING
Art Department Coordinator . . . . .JEREMY BALL
Construction Coordinator. . . . . ZHU BAO SHENG
Construction Forepersons . . . . ZHU GUANG TAI, LI GANG
Special Effects Coordinator. . . . . .KEN DUREY
Special Effects Snow Master . . . . DAGAN JURD
Smoke & Fire Master. . . . . XU REI XIANG
Special Effects Translator . . . . JOEL ROSEN
Special Effects Propmaster . . . . .LIU SHAO CHUN
Assistant Special Effects Propmaster . . . . . . LIU HONG HAI
Assistant Costume Designers LISA FRUCHT, XIE MENG "MEG"
Costume Construction Supervisor . . . . JULIE YRJANSON
China Wardrobe Supervisor. . . . . GUO LEI
Ager/Dyer . . . . ANNA MUNRO

Key Costumers. . . . . HILARY MIEDERER, BAI LU

Beijing Wardrobe Assistants . . . . QI XU DONG, YANG DAN, WU YIN HAO, GUAN JUN, SONG LIN WEI

Wardrobe Coordinator . . . . QIAO JIN FANG

Xinjiang Wardrobe Supervisor. . . . . .ABDULLAH HAPIZ

Xinjiang Wardrobe Assistants .GAI LILI, YANG FANGZHENG, JIANG FENGMEI, SAWUT CHAWAR

Key Makeup Artist. . . . . LESLIE DEVLIN

Makeup Artists. . . . . .WANG XIN "CHRISTIE" ZHANG SHU PING, HUANG PING

Hair Stylist. . . . . FAN YONG JIE "ER GE"

Assistant Hair Stylists . . . . CHE YU, LIU YAN XIA

Beard Makers. . . . . .JIANG CUN, LIANG HAI MAN, GUO XIAO LAN, HU REI, GE XIU MEI, LIU SHU HONG

Happy Pictures Production Manager . . . . . . .MA ZHENG QIANG

Xinjiang Assistant Production Coordinator . . . . . .OMAR OTKUR

China Travel Coordinator. . . . . CHEN YI SONG "SCARLET"

China Production Secretaries. . . . . .LUO SHAN "KATE" ZHOU YUAN

First Assistant Accountant. . . . . .LAURA WILLCOX

Second Assistant Accountant . . . . .KRISTINE BOCHUM

Assistant Accountants . . . . RETHA GELDENHUYS SHAUNA CHO, ZHANG XIU JIN "CANDY", XIONG WEN PING, WAN XU JUAN "JO", DILINUOER

Cashier. . . . . ZHEN XIAO "MICHELLE"

Beijing Location Managers . . . . . PENG RONG, FANG YINCHUN

Xinjiang Assistant Location Manager . . . . KAMIL ZUNUN

Second Second Assistant Director . . . . .ALYSON LATZ

China Additional Assistant Directors. . . . . . . SU HAO QI, LI KAI YIMIGJAN TRDI, PAN YING "STEPHANIE"

Beijing Production Assistants . . . . CHEN XU, YE LU, LI XIAO WANG, SHENG WEN BIN, LU LU, KONG MIN, GOU CHUAN YONG, YAMA RICKY

Xinjiang Production Assistants . . . . KAIYUM, TUDAJI, MIRADEL, KARSYM JIANG

Kashgar Production Office Translator . . . . ELHAM MOHAMMED

Production Assistants. . . . . SUI DONGMING, JILIJIANG YANG HAI BING, MAIYINO KASIMU, PATRICK McDONALD, MIKEY EBERLE, LIU YONG TAO, WANG XIANG, AMWER, LIU DIAN JUN, ELHAM JAN, MA XIN LIN, LU QING LONG, KASEM TURSUN, KYLE JOHNSON, ANDY MORA, ROMAN LUO, JEFF WEIL

Researchers . . . . . SHAHRUKH GRAN, DONNA SAMMANDER RAMEEN MOSHREF JAVID, YAMA RAHIMI

Flying Cam Pilot . . . . EMMANUEL PREVINAIRE

Flying Cam Operator . . . . CHONG SZE KWAN "QUINCY"

Flying Cam Assistant. . . . . MARC ASMODE

Beijing Transportation Captain . . . . LU YU

Xinjiang Transportation Captain . . . . WU ZHEN YUAN

Picture Car Coordinator. . . . . DAVID HARRIS

Beijing Drivers . . ZHANG LEI, TIAN HAI QIANG, WANG BIN, WU XIAN ZHONG, MA JIAN TAO, LIN ZHI QIANG, FENG ZHENG QI, ZHANG LIAN YI, GUO YUN FENG

Xinjiang Drivers . . . . .YOU GUANG SHENG, ABDUKADIR, LI YONG QI, CHEN XING JIANG, ZHANG SHENG XI, WANG HUI, YANG ZHONG ZHI, ZHAO SHENG XIANG, ARKIN A, MA JIAN MIN, ARKIN E, TURSUN, ABDUSATTAR TURDE, ABLIMIT KADER, MIJIT MAHMUT

Mechanic . . . . DI XIAO HONG

Animal Handler . . . . MIJITI

Tutors. . . . . .MOHAMMAD AMAN JOYA, KERRY BOE

Assistant to Mr. Jianxin . . . . CAI XIAO KUI

Medic. . . . . .TONY EVANS

Western Catering & Craft . . . . .CINDY HAMILTON

Chinese Catering . . . . GUO TIAN HE

Visual Effects Assistant . . . . REN CONG "NEO"

Proof Pre-Visualization Lead Artist. . . . . JOTHAM HERZON

Proof Pre-Visualization Artists . . . . ALEXANDER VEGH PARKER SELLERS

AFGHANISTAN UNIT

Kabul Logistical & Travel Support. . . . . .TOLO TELEVISION SAAD MOHSENI, ZAID MOHSENI, JAHID MOHSENI

Production Coordinators. . SEKANDER SALEH, AMIR SHAMIL

Production Support . . . . .SOPHIE BARRY

Casting Associates . . . KRISTY KINNEAR, MUSTAFA HAIDARI

Kabul Casting Support. . . . . FOUNDATION FOR CULTURE AND CIVIL SOCIETY, TIMOR HAKIMYAR

Script Translator. . . . . MARIAM MAHMOUD

POST PRODUCTION

First Assistant Editor . . . . .ALEX OLIVARES

Assistant Editor . . . . .ROBIN GONSALVES

Editorial Translator . . . . NABILA ASLAI

Post Production Supervisor . . . . CAREY LEN SMITH

Post Production Coordinator . . . . LEILANI GUSHIKEN

Post Production Assistant. . . . . .ROB WILSON

Archival Research . . . . .ADELE SPARKS

Supervising Sound Editor . . . . .FRANK EULNER

Sound Designer . . . . STEVE BOEDDEKER

Re-Recording Mixers. . . . . .LORA HIRSCHBERG, MICHAEL SEMANICK

ADR Editors. . . . . GWENDOLYN YATES WHITTLE, MARILYN MCCOPPEN

Dialogue Editors . . . . .MARSHALL WINN, KAREN SPANGENBERG

Assistant Supervising Sound Editor. . . . . ANDRÉ FENLEY

Dialogue / ADR Assistant Editor. . . . . L. CHINO

Foley Artists . JANA VANCE, ELLEN HEUER, DENISE THORPE

Foley Editor. . . . . KEVIN SELLERS

Foley Mixer . . . . .FRANK AGLIERI-RINELLA

Foley Recordist . . . . .SEAN ENGLAND

Mix Technician . . . . TONY SERENO

Recordist . . . . .NATHAN NANCE

Digital Transfer . . . . JONATHAN GREBER CHRISTOPHER BARRON, JOHN COUNTRYMAN

Engineering Services . . . . JIM AUSTIN, DOUG FORD
                                    HOWARD HAMMERMANN
Digital Editorial Services. . . . . DAVID HUNTER
                                     LEFFERT LEFFERTS
ADR Mixer . . . . MICHAEL MILLER
ADR Group Coordinator . . . . L. A. MAD DOGS
Additional Voice . . . . IQBAL THEBA
Re-Recorded at. SKYWALKER SOUND,
             a Lucasfilm Company, Marin County, California
Music Recorded and Mixed by JOSÉ LUIS CRESPO DUEÑAS
Music Editor. JAY B. RICHARDSON
Music Contractors . . . . SANDY De CRESCENT, PETER ROTTER
Music Assistants and Additional Arrangements . JORGE MAGAZ,
                JOSE VILLALOBOS, DAVID CERREJÓN
Music Performed by   THE HOLLYWOOD STUDIO SYMPHONY
Orchestra Conducted by. . . . . MICHAEL NOWAK
Santur, Oud, Lyre of Crete, Rubab. . . . . DIMITRI PSONIS
Bansuri, Ney, Turkish Clarinet. . . . . JAVIER PAXARIÑO
Electric and Acoustic Guitar . . . . JOHN PARSONS
Nylon Guitar . . . . JAVIER CRESPO
Guitar. . . . . HEITOR PEREIRA
Solo Violin . . . . ARA MALIKIAN
Solo Viola. . . . . JULIA MALKOVA
Cello. . . . . MARTIN TILLMAN
Bass . . . . VICTOR MERLO
Snare Drum . . . . ANGEL CRESPO
Alto Flute. . . . . GERI ROTELLA
English Horn and Duduk . . . . CHRIS BLETH
Piano . . . . BRYAN PEZZONE
Harp. . . . . JOANN TUROVSKY
Hand Percussion. . . . . ALEX ACUNA
Tabla. . . . . SATNAM RAMGOTRA
Male Vocal, Ney. . . . . MAJID JAVADI
Female Vocal . . . . SUSSAN DEYHIM
Assistant Engineers . . . . RAUL QUILEZ
               RUBEN SUAREZ, DIEGO BALDUQUE
Music Recorded at . . . . CATA STUDIOS (Madrid)
         WARNER BROS., EASTWOOD SCORING STAGE

XINJIANG SECOND UNIT
Director . . . . REBECCA YELDHAM
Director of Photography . . . . RICHARD BOWEN
First Assistant Director . . . . LAM SUK CHING "SHARON"
Third Assistant Directors . . . . KUER BAN JIANG
          ABUDULI AIZIZE, ABU DOULI, BA YAN
First Assistant Photographer . . . . NGAI MAN YIN
Second Assistant Photographer . . . . WU YONG BO
Set Lighting Technicians . . . . CAO DAWEI, ZHU YANLIN,
          KANG JIANGCHENG, CAO HONGAN
Key Grip. . . . . DENG JUN
Grips. . . . . ANG HAILIANG, FAN YITA, LI XIANG, QI YUE
Wardrobe Supervisor . . . . CAROLINE ESELIN
Kite Assistant. . . . . ALIJAN XIRLAJI

Location Assistant . . . . ABLIMIT
Assistant Hair Stylist . . . . CHE YU
Assistant Makeup Artist. . . . . HUANG PING
Props . . . . ZHANG WEI CHAO, HU YANWU
Video Assist . . . . MATTHEW WAKAI
Assistant Location Manager . . . . MATTHEW WERSINGER
Script Supervisor . . . . REBECCA JIANG
Sound Mixer. . . . . WU LING
Production Coordinator . . . . SABRINA POURCHASSE
Production Associate . . . . FEI WONG
Production Assistants . . . . EKHBAR, ABUDU LUSULI
      SUDEEP MATHUR, ABUDU REYIMU, ABUDU WEILI
Transportation Coordinator . . . . DAVID HARRIS

SAN FRANCISCO UNIT
Art Director . . . . DOUGLAS CUMMING
Production Coordinator . . . . RACHAEL LIN GALLAGHAN
Assistant Production Coordinators . . . . . . SHARLENE F. DUALE
      DIONNE LOTIVIO, CHRISTOPHER BENNETT
First Assistant Accountant . . . . RYAN WHAN
Payroll Accountant. . . . . DAVID HICKEY
Art Department Coordinator . . . . MAYA OWINGS
Art Department Production Assistant . . . . MICHELE KITAGAWA
A Second Assistant Photographer. . . . . MARK GILMER
B Camera Operator . . . . SIMON JAYES
B First Assistant Photographer . . . . DON STEINBERG
B Second Assistant Photographer. . . . . KENNY BAZAL, JR.
Film Loader. . . . . COURTNEY L. HARRELL
Casting . . . . NINA HENNINGER
Background Casting. . . . . SARAH KLIBAN
Catering . . . . GALA CATERING
Construction Coordinator. . . . . BEN NICHOLS
Lead Painter . . . . DALE HAUGO
On-Set Painter . . . . TOM RICHARDSON
Craft Service . . . . SANDY REED
Lead Greens . . . . JAMES BURKE
Key Grip. . . . . DON L. HENDERSON
Grips. . . . . BROOK JOHNSON, BRAD MARTINEZ,
      GREG CHILDERS, IAN CHRISS, J. CHUCK BIAGIO
          JOSEPH J. ALLEN, TOBY LAWRENCE
Hair Department Head. . . . . JENNIFER TREMONT
Key Hair Stylist . . . . YVETTE RIVAS
Makeup Artist. GRETCHEN DAVIS
Location Manager . . . . ERNEST BELDING
Assistant Location Managers. . . . . FELIX GEHM
      MATTHEW RIUTTA, PETER MOODY
Property Master . . . . PATRICK LUDDEN
Assistant Property Master . . . . ANNIE MUELLER
Props . . . . GRETCHEN SCHARFENBERG
Lead Person . . . . JOHN MICHELETOS
Set Dressers . . . . . . LAWERENCE HORNBECK, MIKE HELBIG,
      PETER HUDSON, DAN MOLNAR, LOU VISCO,
                LEIGHANNE HADDOCK

Set Costumers .... VALERIE WHITE, KATHLEEN GIORDANO DEIRDRE SCULLY
Set Lighting Technicians ....CHRIS SHELLENBERGER JEFF GILLIAM, SPENCER MULCAHY, ZACH LOVE, DAN C. FERREIRA, MARK NAKAHARA
Production Sound Mixer .... NELSON STOLL
Boom Operator.....................BRIAN COPENHAGEN
Utility Sound .... STEPHEN BALLIET
Special Effects Coordinator .... THOMAS F. SINDICICH
Production Assistants..................... JEFF KRAMER, JENNIFER JOURDAN, AARON C. FITZGERALD MATT LAKE, JAMIE L. GAINES, JIM SERCHAK NATASCHA DIMITRIJEVIC, ANTONIO G. GRAÑA, RAM-SAY WILLIAMS
Studio Teacher ....BONNIE HUDSON
Transportation Captain.......................DON FEENEY
Transportation Co-Captain..............FRANKLIN J. ROCHA
Drivers .... TONY DINGMAN, BOB BARBOSA, CHRIS DEGUZMAN, JOHN BRADLEY, JOHN BROMSTEAD, JR., TOMMY RIZZO, TONY PONTECORVO, WILLIAM J. ROGERS, WILLIE BROCK
Video Assist ....JOHN TRUNK
Visual Effects by .... CAFÉ FX INC.
Visual Effects Supervisor....................DAVID EBNER
Visual Effects Producer ....LES G. JONES
Animation Lead .... LEIF EINARSSON
Animators..............RON FRIEDMAN, NEIL LIM SANG, JASON THIELEN, VINCENT DELAY, OMRA MENKES
Matte Painters .... LEI JIN, DYLAN COLE, REN CONG, BRANDON KACHEL
2D Plate Reconstruction .... LINDSAY ANDERSON
Rotoscoping...............................EDDIE SORIA
Compositing Lead .... ROBIN GRAHAM
Compositors..................ED MENDEZ, CHRIS PINTO, RICHARD REED, JEFF ARNOLD, SEAN COONCE
2D Artist .... CHRIS BALL
3D Modeling/Texturing .. STEVE ARGUELLO, MIKE FISCHER, JOE HOBACK, GARBRIEL VARGAS, TIM ALEXANDER, ALEX FRIDERICI, STEVE HUTCHINS, OLEK LYZWANSKI
Massive Crowds............................TIM LeDOUX
3D Lighting Lead..........................TODD PERRY
3D Matchmovers .... KEVIN HOPPE, ANDY BYRNE FATIMA MOJADIDDY
Visual Effects Managing Editor................ DESI R. ORTIZ
Visual Effects Editors.... KEVIN LaNEAVE, LIBOR ZEDNICEK
Visual Effects Coordinator..............MARTY HOLTHAUS
Visual Effects Production Assistant...... SHANNON KRUEGER
Data I/O ....CALEB KIRBY
Rendering.........BRIAN OPENSHAW, SAY RINTHARAMY
Production Executives ....JEFF BARNES, O. D. WELCH
Executive Producer .... VICKI GALLOWAY WEIMER
Opticals & Digital Film Recording .....LASER PACIFIC MEDIA CORPORATION, a Kodak Company

DI Colorist ....MIKE SOWA
Color Science..............................DOUG JAQUA
DI Project Managers .... NANCY FULLER, JAKE RICE MIKE BROSIUS
Digital Data Management ... VINCE LAVARES, JEFF CHARLES
Digital Data Conform .... VALANCE EISLEBEN, STACY UNDERHILL, PAUL GRENVILLE, CARRIE OLIVER
Digital Subtitle Compositing .... WILLIAM MISSETT MICHAEL CASTILLO
DI Editorial .... LINDA WILLIAMS
Camera Cranes & Dollies by .... CHAPMAN/LEONARD STUDIO EQUIPMENT, INC.
Main Title Design MK12
End Titles by .... PACIFIC TITLE ART & DESIGN
Color Timer .... HARRY MULLER

Produced With Assistance Of CHINA FILM CO-PRODUCTION CORPORATION AND BEIJING HAPPY PICTURES CULTURAL COMMUNICATIONS CO., LTD.

Produced With Assistance Of MR. HUANG JIANXIN

The Producers Wish To Thank:
CHINA FILM BUREAU
CHINA SOUTHERN AIRLINES
CITY AND COUNTY OF KASHGAR, XINJIANG
CITY AND COUNTY OF TASHKORGAN, XINJIANG
THE UYGUR COMMUNITY OF THE AUTONOMOUS REGION OF XINJIANG
AFGHAN FILM
RADIO TELEVISION AFGHANISTAN
CENTER FOR AFGHAN STUDIES, UNIVERSITY OF NE-BRASKA
SIDDIQ BARMAK
MOHSEN MAKHMALBAF
AHMAD LATIF
JIM BURROUGHS
SUZANNE BAUMAN
ADRIAN BELIC
BAHAUDIN MUJTABA
NAZI ETEMADI
PROFESSOR LORRAINE SAKATA
DANA KOHLER
RENEE CHABRIA

Special Thanks HANS ZIMMER

THE MAGNIFICENT SEVEN CLIP
Courtesy of ©1960 Metro-Goldwyn-Mayer Studios, Inc.
All Rights Reserved.

STEVE McQUEEN Performance
Courtesy of ©2007 Steve McQueen™ Licensed by
Chadwick McQueenand the Terry McQueen Testamentary Trust,
Represented by Corbis®.

Filmed at:
KASHGAR AND TASHKORGAN, XINJIANG, CHINA
BEIJING, CHINA AND
SAN FRANCISCO, CALIFORNIA

Social Action Campaign
www.participate.net

Soundtrack on EDGE

SONGS

AYE DARA KAY JAYLAWNI
Traditional

TANHA SHUDAM TANHA
Written & Performed by Ahmad Zahir
Courtesy of Shabnam Zahir

PALOMA BLANCA
Written by Johannes Bouwens
Performed by George Baker Selection
Courtesy of EMI Music Netherlands BV
Under license from EMI Film & Television Music

EL BIMBO
Written by Claude Ganem, Performed by Ehsan Aman

AZ MAN BEGUREZED
Written & Performed by Ahmad Zahir
Courtesy of Shabnam Zahir

YADI ROZGARI SHEREEM
Written & Performed by Ahmad Zahir
Courtesy of Shabnam Zahir

SARE NAAR AAMADAEM
Written & Performed by Farhad Darya

BEDS ARE BURNING
Written by Peter Garrett, Peter Gifford, Robert Hirst
and James Moginie, Performed by Midnight Oil
Courtesy of Columbia Records and Sony BMG Music
Entertainment (Australia) Pty.
By arrangement with Sony BMG Music Entertainment

KISS ME DEADLY
Written by Mick Smiley, Performed by Lita Ford
Courtesy of The RCA Records Label
By arrangement with Sony BMG Music Entertainment

DUK DUK
Arranged by Khaled Kayhan, Performed by Fawad Ramez
Licensed courtesy of Kayhan Studios

JADOO KARDEI JANA
Written by Trana Saz, Performed by Haider Salim
Courtesy of Cinevision Studio

TAUTA WYUM YOW AWHANG
Written & Performed by Yar Mohammad and Homa Afghanmeena

OMAID e MAN
Written & Performed by Ehsan Aman

ASTA BERO
Written & Performed by Ehsan Aman

DUKHTARE DARYA
Written & Performed by Ehsan Aman

AN UGLY FACT OF LIFE from FRIDAY NIGHT LIGHTS
Written by Christopher Hrasky, Michael James, Munaf Rayani &
Mark Smith
Performed by Explosions In The Sky
Courtesy of Universal Studios LLLP

GRAN AFGHAN NAGHMA
Written & Performed by Quraishi

SUPPLICATION
Written by Sami Yusuf and Bara Kherigi
Performed by Sami Yusuf
Courtesy of Awakening Records

Camera Credit
FILMED WITH ARRI™ CAMERAS & LENSES

Prints by DELUXE, AVID, KODAK

Dolby® Digital In Selected Theatres

DTS™ Sound In Selected Theatres

SDDS Sony Dynamic Digital Sound™ In Selected Theatres

MPAA # 43592   I.A.T.S.E.

159

Acknowledgments

The publisher wishes to thank the following for their special contributions to the book:

At Sidney Kimmel Entertainment: Bill Horberg and Chantal Nong; Rebecca Yeldham; at DreamWorks: Christine Birch; Elaine Koster, Chandler Crawford, Jody Hotchkiss; at Paramount Vantage: President John Lesher, Creative Director Adam Kassan, Co-Head of Marketing Megan Colligan, Co-Head of Marketing Guy Endore-Kaiser, and in the Marketing, Publicity, and Licensing Departments: Lindsay Frank, Julie Tustin, Healey Young, Crystal Shin, April Syrek, Dino Bruce, Alison Lehrer, Fay Smith, Chrissy Gaffney, and Risa Kessler.

Also, at ABC Carpet: Vice Chairman Graham Head, Senior Executive Vice President Alex Kimia, and Public Relations Manager Angela Gruszka; at Café FX: Chris Slaughter; and at Ignition Print: Tawny Wolfe.

And, of course, Khaled Hosseini for his personal foreword, David Benioff for his wonderful adaptation, and Marc Forster for his artful direction and special assistance.